I Change, I Change

Poems by Barbara Deming

photo by Jack Sennott
Barbara Deming 1934-35

I Change, I Change

Poems
by Barbara Deming

EDITED AND WITH AN INTRODUCTION

BY JUDITH MCDANIEL

PREFACE BY GRACE PALEY

Published by New Victoria Publishers Inc., a non-profit feminist, literary, and cultural organization, PO Box 27, Norwich, VT 05055-0027.

Cover Painting © Georgina Forbes
Back cover photo of Judith McDaniel by Tee A. Corrine

Printed and Bound in the USA
1 2 3 4 5   2000 1999 1998 1997 1996

Library of Congress Cataloging-in-Publication Data

Deming, Barbara, 1917-
    I change, I change : poems / Barbara Deming.
        p. cm.
    ISBN 0-934678-72-3   ISBN 0-934678-79-0
    1. Lesbians -- Poetry. I. Title.
PS3554.E47512 1996
811' .54--dc20   95-26693
                                       CIP

CONTENTS

WITH THANKS

This book would not have been published without the efforts of Vida Ginsberg Deming, who believed it should happen, and Beth Dingman of New Victoria Publishers, who wanted to return a favor to Barbara Deming. I am grateful to both for their dedication, generosity, and good will.

I thank Vida Ginsberg Deming, Mary Meigs, Anne Poor, and Emily Alford for the hours they have spent talking with me about their relationships with Barbara Deming. I thank Blue Lunden for her continuing support for my work as Barbara Deming's literary executor and for her reflections on Barbara's life and work.

Barbara's three brothers, MacDonald, Quentin, and Angus Deming have also been good-humored and gracious with their time and memories as I interviewed each of them.

Minnie Bruce Pratt was a thoughtful reader and her perspective on Barbara's poetry informed my own.

My own personal thanks to my partner Jan for her love and encouragement and accurate critique.

I believe Barbara would have wanted to dedicate this book to her partner Jane (Verlaine) Gapen. Hence—

in loving memory of Jane, unique spirit, beloved
partner of Barbara, this book is offered.

Photo © Judith McDaniel
Peace encampment 1983

PREFACE

by Grace Paley

It's hard as one grows older to remember—not so much events, as when—in what year of what life—they occurred. Luckily—for people who have been politically active—there are the FBI reports available for little cost. From these you can learn the important dates of your life as well as the day you were one in a hundred-thousand at some demonstration, standing at the back of the crowd near the home-going bus, eating a pretzel.

There I saw the extraordinary dates—the long three days I spent with the poet Barbara Deming in 1970, in two or three holding areas while the May Day demonstration seethed outside our vision or hearing. We talked about everything, even poetry, but not the fact that Barbara was a poet.

In her presence, her attentiveness, her intelligent and lovely speech, she was, clearly a poet-woman, but it was many years before I knew her written down work. In those years of the rise and solidification of the feminist movement and lesbian liberation struggles, she gave herself the task of articulating the acts of those movements, their theoretical and practical importance in connecting the personal liberations to the civil rights and anti-war years. In long letters she labored to open the dear minds of her old comrades. Meanwhile she inspired the young women who appeared just in time (they felt) to announce themselves and take non-violent action in their communal defense. It isn't always the truth that makes us free. It is often speaking the truth that frees us, or at least teaches that we have allowed shadows of cultural oppression to lie, even lightly, across our political and literary work.

The May Day walk and Demonstration against our American War in Vietnam began. Barbara and I had joined the War Resisters League. One of our objects would be to obstruct traffic, to stop the city in which men in meetings, in war rooms, and probably at dinner—planned the devastation of Vietnam. It seemed a mild thing really to tie up some traffic. For some reason, Barbara and I holding hands decided to act at once. We walked out into the moving road and sat down in the midst of cars whose drivers in a tire-squealing, cursing rage thought it was better *not* to kill us. I think we both felt a little foolish since the purpose of direct action is to confront the opposing citizen, give him or her time to think, not necessarily achieve one's own sudden death. So we did feel particularly foolish (especially me) since we were arrested immediately and missed most of the three day actions.

These elicited a panicky response from the Nixon government which gathered up fifteen-hundred people, some of them tourists and jailed them.

At first we were sequestered in a football field, soon joined by a couple hundred other demonstrators. We were impressed by the immediate construction of a latrine at one end and the creation of a kind of tarpaulin shelter by some young men with camping experience. The sun in its compulsive way abandoned us (we were personalizing a little by then). Overhead helicopters with our representatives and senators were hovering. They had been told we were cold and hadn't eaten. This was not exactly true since most of us had lots of carrots in our backpacks. Barbara and I arm and arm keeping each other warm, walked and talked mostly about the deepening struggle in our own anti-war movement. We also talked about sexual love, commitment, life companions and the young people around us whose major slogan shouted often during the three days was "Fuck that shit!"

Suddenly the gates opened and a couple of concerned legislators appeared among us. And there was our own New York representative Bella Abzug for whom we felt a common affection, even admiration, with whom we had major disagreements about strategies and bottom line theories on how to act and end the war.

She asked us how we were. "Great," we said or something like that, "But a lot of people are really cold," we said as though we were not.

"Yes, I see." Then she walked up and down the field, talking to others, telling about the number of arrests happening outside our outdoor enclosure. She returned to us. By that time we were visibly cold. "Well, Barbara, well Grace, " she said grinning, " I guess you're where you want to be and I'm where I want to be."

Then we all laughed because it was certainly true. Barbara and I lived the next couple of days removed to the warmer indoor stadium now among maybe five-hundred people, students, friends, able to call or be part of wider meetings, listening, listening. Barbara's gift—listening.

I want to end with the poemness of Barbara Deming. In 1984 Barbara was dying of ovarian cancer. She said, "I don't want to die in a chaos of numbness and nausea. I'm serene now. I want to die in that serenity." She said this to me in the course of a long telephone conversation. She had returned to Sugarloaf Key to be with her companion Jane Gapen and the other women of that community. After her death our friend Blue brought me two little wool hats Barbara wanted me to have. She also left me an envelope with pebbles and shards from her journey to the villages of Vietnam at war. On the envelope in trembling script she'd written "endless love…" not "*with* endless love," that would have been personal. Endless love with these stones from the streets of another peoples whose great suffering at our country's hands we had a common remembrance. I keep that envelope where I can see it and touch the stones. They speak to me with the special straightforwardness of metaphor: Do not forget. Tell that story again and again.

Barbara Deming
July 23, 1917–
August 2, 1984

Program Cover: Friends Meeting House
Florida November 17th, 1984
Photographs and credits: (from the back of the program)
Bobbie about 16 years old photographer unknown
1935 /Jack Sennott
Portraits: 1944 and in the 50s / Consuelo Kanaga
With cats: 1979 / Louise Bernikow
At home, December, 1981 / JEB (Joan E. Biren)
Upper right corner: At the Seneca Encampment, August 4, 1983 JEB
Lower left corner: On trial, Waterloo, NY,August 3, 1983 / JEB

Designer: Nancy Johnson

THE WOMEN SHE LOVED

Poems and Conversations
An Introduction by Judith McDaniel

Barbara Deming. Writer. Activist for peace, civil rights, feminism, and lesbian and gay rights. When I asked her, shortly before her death, how she would like to be remembered, her reply came swiftly and without thought. "As a poet," she said. "That first. Always."

Why did she write poetry? "For most of my life I have intermittently written poems— because they rose in me to be written. I never particularly questioned what made me write them." As a young woman of sixteen, the poems "just came pouring out, bursting out," and that is obvious in the first section of this manuscript. As a result, she mused in 1982, perhaps it is "my sexual self who is my poet....My sexual self and my rebel self, I might say. For were not the two born together?"[1]

When she died, she left this manuscript, rough typed with hand-noted corrections. Often a question mark sat next to a line she had been struggling with. Dozens of copies of each poem existed in her files, revised again and again, sometimes with only a single word or form of a word changed—and this in the days before computers when any change meant a retyping.

It is surely fair to say that Barbara Deming never gained her wish—to be remembered as a poet. Most readers who are familiar with her work know her first from *Prison Notes*, an account of her struggles during the civil rights movement when she was arrested and jailed in Albany, Georgia. We know her as one of the foremost advocates of nonviolence in the long struggle against nuclear arms and war. Some may remember her from *Revolution and Equilibrium*, which recounts her trip to Hanoi during the height of

1

the U.S. bombing of that city. Others first knew Barbara Deming's writing when they read *We Cannot Live Without Our Lives*, an early book about feminism that was published in 1974 and dedicated "to my lesbian sisters." And women who were at the Seneca Women's Peace Encampment in upstate New York in the summer of 1983 may remember Barbara Deming herself as she walked from the Seneca Falls Women's Hall of Fame toward the Army Depot, was stopped—with many other women—on a bridge in Waterloo, was arrested with fifty-four other women and thus became one of the "Jane Doe's" of the Peace Encampment. But few remember that Barbara Deming also wrote poetry.

I myself am a poet and a lesbian. As I think about Barbara Deming's life and work, as I think about her desire to be "known" as a poet and about the reality that her political writing—not her poetry—was where we find the passion in her work, I find two thematic areas I need to explore. The first area has to do with that phenomenon known to lesbian and gay poets: the closet. What does it mean to us as artists when we cannot openly be who we are in our work? The second is the question of what it means to be a poet in a time and a place when art and politics are considered irreconcilable, when politics is not deemed a fit subject for art.

After her first juvenile poems, exuberant and celebratory poems about the rewards and pains of love, Barbara Deming's poetry became more formal. As a reader, I sometimes have difficulty finding the emotional focus of her poem. When I looked through Barbara's journals, letters, and papers as I prepared to write the story of her life, I found many occasions on which it was clear that she had shown her honest and exuberant early poems to others; and either Barbara was told the poems were not good or she was able to sense the reader's discomfort with the poems without knowing exactly the cause of it. One result was to make Barbara shy of sharing her poems with anyone. When I interviewed her friend, the poet James Merrill, he told me how helpful Barbara's editorial eye had been to him as a young poet. He sent her poems which she critiqued and rearranged in a volume which then "made much more sense," according to Merrill. "And did you read Barbara's poems?" I asked him. "Oh, no," he replied. "I don't remember ever seeing her poems in manuscript, except when I accepted some of them for *Voices*," the literary magazine he was editing in the 1950s.[2]

I have to wonder whether Barbara felt more comfortable sending poems to James Merrill's literary journal in the first place because she knew he was a gay man. But even then, the risk she took with Merrill was very slim, sending him only the poems she felt sure of, and not many of those.

One way a less experienced poet improves is by letting others read her poems, by listening to what readers have to say, and finally by developing that elusive faculty of self-evaluation—the ability to sift through responses and find those that are useful, those that fit the poem. Many poets are never able to distinguish in this way and never grow in their work as a consequence; but if something in the environment keeps them from ever engaging in that first step, if the subject of their poem, for example, is about a woman loving another woman—and that is forbidden—how much harder is it for the poet to risk herself in a public way. And without the risk, there can be no growth as an artist.

Granted, there have been lesbian poets of Barbara Deming's generation who remained closeted and still published outstanding work. "Bed of forbidden things," wrote Muriel Rukeyser, "finally known—"[3] Elizabeth Bishop. May Swenson. Others not yet named. All concealed their sexual relationships with other women, and yet some of these became "known" as poets.

In the social world that surrounded Barbara's life, however, to be an artist of any description meant removing oneself from political interactions. Muriel Rukeyser was born into a Jewish/left/worker tradition that allowed her to write about World War II, about visiting a Korean dissident in prison. In Barbara Deming's tradition, the artist did art. The businessman did business, the politician did politics. To be an artist who was engaged in the work of the world did not compute. And so we do not find her writing poems that reflect the civil rights movement, none that comment on the Vietnam War, none that are about nonviolence or disarmament or the nuclear threat she worked against.

Instead, when Barbara began to interest herself in politics and protesting against nuclear weapons, her partner at the time, Mary

Meigs, was personally threatened by Barbara's political involvement. "Because I already felt guilty about my life as an artist, because it cut me off from what was going on in the world....That was the life of an artist. I'd embraced that life and I liked it."[4] The assumption that being an artist cut one off from what was going on in the world may have been more difficult for Barbara as a poet than her experience of being closeted.

* * *

Barbara carefully divided this manuscript into eight sections, seven named after women she had loved, complete with dates, and one section named after the family home on South Mountain Road in New City, New York, just across the river from Manhattan. The manuscript itself was an affirmation—Barbara's final uncloseting.[5]

Norma. Casey. Emmie. Vida. Annie. Mary. Jane. She loved and pursued all seven women. Five were Barbara's lovers, and three were also her partners in established relationships. None recall ever discussing Barbara's own poetry with her while it was in process. She could not even share drafts of her poems with her lovers. The revisions she puzzled over with cramped notes in the margins were alterations she suggested to herself. Poetry, for Barbara Deming, remained always a very private event.

In her friendships, intense conversation and the ability to listen with riveted attention to another person were the hallmarks of Barbara Deming. Poetry seems to have been one of the ways that Barbara made friends with herself, listened to herself, talked to herself, considered her world and her place in it.

The poems about her life on South Mountain Road describe Barbara in the context of her family and are pivotal in understanding how poetry functioned in her life. Born in 1917, Barbara was the second of four children and the only girl. Her mother was Katherine Burritt who had been a singer before her marriage. Katherine's childhood home had been defined by the tension between her artistic, music teacher father, and her practical business woman mother—a tension she seemed to have reproduced in her own family life when she, the singer, married lawyer Harold Deming.

Young Barbara apparently saw her parents in this light, even though her father, Harold, was a poet and painter, a man who appreciated the arts in many forms. Harold was also a naturalist who would have loved to follow that direction, but his father determined that he would be a lawyer.[6] Nonetheless, his children seemed most affected by Harold's formality and rigid ethical codes. "Remember," Barbara reminded herself about going down to dinner in her parent's house, "Elbows off the table, eyes/ in front! One must be a poet only in one's own/ room."[7] No slouching at her father's table and no other "deviations" were allowed in her father's home either; there was no space, Barbara felt, for the poet or the rebel. At the same time, these poems and all of Barbara's later poems reflect the ways in which her father's love of the natural world imprinted on Barbara. The primary imagery in her poetry is from nature. Whether a long reflection on one of the cats she lived with or a detailed observation of the way ducks take flight off the water, Barbara's eye saw nature rather than civilization as the source of her inspiration. Fortunately, nature, unlike politics, was an acceptable subject for poetry.

Harold's letters to Barbara *were* always concerned and loving, but they *were* the letters of a father who knows what is best for his child. He wanted Barbara to get a teaching job, something secure, something firm. She had no interest in teaching, she wanted to write, but earning a living as a writer? He could have supported her while she established herself, but he refused. Harold Deming's own father had insisted that all of his children, including his daughters, would be educated and would work to support themselves. Harold insisted on the same. Barbara futilely pled her case:

> I have heard you remark that you do not believe in parents giving their children incomes, because it is not good for them. Now in general I agree with this, in many cases, that is, that it effects no good. But I think this is not always so. In my case I know for example that if I had a million dollars I would still find work a necessity—because it is only when I work that I can be happy. [8]

Harold did not relent. Barbara's decision to go to graduate school the following year did not ease the tension between father and daughter. Barbara was set on going to Louisiana State

University to work with Robert Penn Warren on *The Southern Review*. In another letter to her father, Barbara told him that she feels in sympathy with *The Southern Review*, that the editors "see human values running into the sand and they find an approach to literature one way of reasserting these values."[9] Harold couldn't imagine "that a place called Louisiana State University could possibly have anything of intellectual merit worth his daughter's participation or his helping financially with it."[10] And so, Harold forbade it. She could go to Case Western Reserve. And did, spending the following year, 1940-1941, taking a Master's degree in Drama and Theater. When she was ready to graduate, the struggle continued—the life of the artist or the secure life of a teacher? Harold finally conceded that a compromise might be art criticism or editing:

> My well-known Holland Dutch obstinacy makes my mind revert to the idea which I had a year or two ago, that a critical or editing job with a publishing house or a magazine right here in New York would furnish you the most hopeful road toward what would in the long run bring you the greatest happiness. Such a job would, I believe, take considerably less out of you than a teaching job, and thus leave some energy free for creative writing during your off hours.[11]

Barbara seems to have agreed. She at least began to look for editorial work, writing to one publisher, "My own writing I intend to pursue. I make slow headway here, however, and I do not wish to seek my living by it. I look most seriously, therefore, towards obtaining some sort of editorial, or related, work."[12] By 1942 she had a job at the Museum of Modern Art as a film analyst/critic on the Library of Congress Film Project. She worked at this until the project expired in 1945, earning at her peak the munificent sum of $50 a week. [13] Even her father must have been pleased.

In the meantime, Barbara lived other parts of her life on parallel tracks, as many children do. As a young woman, she graduated from the Friends Seminary of the Fifteenth Street Quaker Meeting in New York City. She went to Bennington College, worked summers in a stock company she and some friends started in the town of Bennington. These things her father knew about, but her inner life was unknown to him. He would not have known that she sometimes dressed in her brother's clothes and went out in the world to see how it felt. Nor that she had given herself a secret name, Slian Laeth. Her father was certainly unaware when she began a passionate affair with her family's neighbor Norma Millay while she was still a high school student, but her mother knew. Barbara wrote love poems to Norma and long letters about her passion to her mother who was wintering in Florida. In one letter, written from the family's home in Manhattan, she told her mother,

> Norma has been staying in town this week with us. We've been seeing the town. We went to a play Monday night—The Green Bay Tree. Oh, mummy, it's such fun going places with her. She's well— well I guess you know. I worship her—and mummy, she really likes me. I can never truly believe it. Oh, we've talked and—oh, I love her, I love her, I love her. [14]

The poems from this year before college are passionate, exuberant, and fairly unschooled and unstructured. The breathless quality of "she held the flower cold up against her cheek" reminds us that young Barbara Deming lived in the same village as the celebrated e.e. cummings ("songs less firm than your body's whitest song.")[15] In the best tradition of youthful imitation, Barbara's poems experimented with capitalization, line arrangements, punctuation, and other grammatical and structural forms. At this point in her development, she seems much less influenced by the formalism of Edna St. Vincent Millay, although two of the poems in this section tell of her passionate wait to meet the famous poet and the anti-climactic event—which in its cool irony does in fact pay tribute to Millay's voice.

In another letter, written to her mother that winter from the South Mountain Road country home, Barbara confesses, "I go for walks. I walk up to Norma's mailbox and touch it and come back." She wishes she had someone to talk to, "but you're away—and the only person besides you I'd think of talking to is Bessie—she'd call me a nut (which I suppose I am) and make me feel better—but she's away too."[16] Bessie Breuer had been a friend of Katherine Deming's before Katherine's marriage to Harold. Their daughters, Anne and Barbara, were about the same age.

Bessie was a writer who had worked for her living since she was a young woman, becoming an editor—the first woman in such a position—at the *Herald Tribune* in her twenties. Later she published novels and short stories in *The New Yorker* which established her reputation as a serious writer. Her husband was the painter Henry Varnum Poor, and their home on South Mountain Road was a haven for writers and artists like Truman Capote, Lotte Lenya and Kurt Weil, and photographer Consuelo Kanaga. As a teenager, Barbara was drawn to the more relaxed atmosphere of Bessie's home and to Bessie's professionalism. While Barbara's mother Katherine had been a singer as a young woman, it was not a career commitment that carried on past her marriage. One suspects that young Barbara knew at an early age that marriage was not going to be the way she supported herself. According to Bessie's daughter Anne Poor, "Bobbie [Barbara's name in her family] adopted my mother and my mother adopted Bobbie. They sat together for years going over my mother's manuscripts, every comma, every this, every that."[17] Barbara valued this time with Bessie in many ways, but her professional resume for 1946 is especially revealing, listing as it does, "Private editorial work for Bessie Breuer, novelist—at various times over the past ten years—$8 a day."[18] In one of the poems in the South Mountain Road section, when she felt she had lost her direction as a writer, Barbara wrote: "As I walked back from talk with my writer friend,/ felt as though I could see again….There is so much that/ has not been seen by each of us."[19] Each of the poems that follows takes up a theme from the conversation with Bessie. It was Bessie who helped Barbara keep on track at this time in her life, rediscover her lost sight, her direction.

* * *

When Barbara left for Bennington College in the fall of 1934, she was a poet who had won the Friends Academy Prize and seen her first work in print, she was a young woman who had experienced a passionate affair with an older woman, and she came from a home where resistance to her father was the key to becoming who she wanted to be. In her stubbornness, her iron-willed determination, in her sense of knowing that she knew the right way, Barbara was more like her father than she was ever willing to admit.[20] In her easy, open sexuality, and her passion for intensity, she resembled her mother. Vida Deming, Barbara's sister-in-law, remembers Barbara falling "madly in love with men and with women....Being in love was terribly important. In that period between the wars there was a kind of deification of being in love, of romantic love, which she grew up with."[21]

At Bennington Barbara met four of the women whose names became chapters in this retrospective book: Casey, Emmie, Vida, and Jane. In Barbara's first letters home, she writes about one of her new friends, who was probably third year student, Dorothy Case (O'Brian) or Casey, a "zippy girl" who didn't keep within the polite limits. She also writes about poet Genevieve Taggard whose most well known book, *The Life and Mind of Emily Dickinson*, was published in 1930, just before she began teaching at Bennington. Taggard was a socialist whose poems appeared in *The Liberator* and *The Masses*. Impressed, but not awed by her surroundings, young Barbara tells her mother:

> o baby je hav just met genevieve taggard and she is swell darling she is going to be my adviser i think and she is swell darling....im majoring in verse writing with taggard and im not sure yet whether to do straight studio work in painting....o mummy i have two swell friends this zippy girl whos a friend of wallys baby....shes grand and swell to talk to because shes very honest and has very mature points of view also she has very much the same attitude i have toward things....a lot of the girls up here are really rather childish.[22]

We can assume that one of the things Barbara found more "mature" about Dorothy Case was her sexuality. Easily bisexual, according to the women who knew her well, Casey was Barbara's lover intermittently during Barbara's years at Bennington. Neither woman limited her sexual expression—both had other lovers, male and female, during those years. Vida Ginsberg [Deming], who arrived at Bennington just in time for Barbara's last year of college, remembers Casey from summer stock theater as a handsome, black-eyed, sophisticated woman.[23]

However long and however seriously Barbara and Casey were lovers, the friendship endured during college. Intense, self-exploring letters during the times when they were apart are testimony to the depth of their communication. At the end of the summer of

1937, as she was beginning her last year at Bennington, Barbara wrote to Casey about where to go, what to do after graduation. She believed she shouldn't go back home.

> you see my family is so goddam good to me it's bad. the real point is if I stay around home I'll begin to forget who's who. it is really my mother I have to scram from whom god knows I love dearly and never was mother less tyrannical but can you see any point to it when I say that if I stuck around home I would begin I know to not hate her ever but kind of flinch when our elbows met? which would be no fault of hers but it is for many reasons all centered on the fact that I am her body once removed and there was a period when I so almost identified myself with my mother and clad myself in her burdens (which I distorted, being adolescent) and this I no longer do and her burdens whatever they are are her own business and mine mine but it is still impossible to be completely objective.

Barbara saw also in herself "a tendency toward martyrdom, a kind of hypochondria, a perverse pleasure in being imposed upon, dramatizing myself afflicted and teeth grit smilingly." She saw these traits primarily in her maternal grandmother, but also in her mother (though "very slight in her") and wanted to root them out of her own personality. Bessie, she told Casey, is so good for her because she finds herself hardened and nourished by Bessie, "because though she may praise me yet she also clarified my faults and weaknesses and she praises me as of potential too not as actual, therefore sets me toward the future." She ended the letter by saying it "is so helpful to write it to you and kind of get it all clear to myself which I am just beginning to see."[24]

The poems Barbara wrote during this period reflect this introspective side of her. "I have taken my heart out tinily/ to contemplate," she writes, and contemplate it she does—both heart and body, for the two seem quite irrevocably connected at this time in her life. Her introspection reveals clearly both her passionate sensuality and her willingness to encounter the pain that all too often went along with such openness. She was, after all, a poet, and for the poet in Barbara, "there is this awareness of pain."

Here in these college poems, Barbara gave us the first accounts of betrayal and, it is possible to assume, homophobia. In "The

Taunt"[25] she flees a woman who has rejected her sexual advances, who laughed at the thought of such a thing and at Barbara. Probably not a poem about Casey, this poem is nevertheless an important addition to this section as a reminder that the real—homophobic—world was present, even in the secluded walks and paths of Bennington, Vermont.

It is not possible to tell from the dates on Barbara's revision of her poems when she began to experiment with changing female pronouns to male in order to accommodate the "real world," but it did happen while she was at Bennington. Some of them are ludicrous when changed, like "he held the flower cold up against his cheek." Other changes were more elaborate, adding entire sections to create a male listener to whom the woman in the poem is speaking.

In one letter home to her mother, Barbara told about going to a reading by Robert Frost. In another, she wrote about hearing Padraic Colum speak and then going over to Genevieve Taggards' with Casey "and a couple of other kids in this irish course" to talk for several hours. Yet another letter told her mother how she hopes they can get poet Wallace Stevens to come and read. With the exception of Taggard as a mentor and influence, Barbara did not mention any women poets in these letters.

Barbara remembered, writing in 1982, that while she did not tell her mentor Bessie Breuer about her affair with Norma, she did show her some of the early poems about being in love. She also showed those poems to Casey and to Taggard. Taggard's response, according to Barbara, was that she didn't "like this kind of poem"and introduced Barbara to poets like Auden, and presumably Robert Frost, Padraic Colum, and Wallace Stevens. One result was that Barbara's poems stopped "pouring out." She had the urge to write, but the process "became more laborious." Another teacher during those years, Wallace Fowlie, told her that her poems "lacked sincerity," a judgment Barbara agreed with when she looked back at work like "The Tragedian."

On the whole, however, Barbara remembered her years at Bennington as a "wonderful free experience" and that she and her classmates saw each other as "beautiful and talented." Graduation was hard. The year was 1938. The United States was in the middle of the depression and, although the war in Europe was still being fought by others, Barbara was profoundly aware of it. References to Barcelona, bombs, Verdun, barbed wire, the bombing of civilians threaded through her awareness during her last semester at Bennington—at the same time she was taking a Shakespeare course with Frances Fergusson and costume design in the theater department. Her friend Anne Poor remembers "the morning Barbara and I, leaving the Commons Building at Bennington, opened up the *N.Y. Times* and there covering the whole front page was the news report of this unthinkable horror," the indiscriminate bombing of civilians in the city of Barcelona.[26]

The uncertainty of life in the "real world," with all of its questions about income and occupation, was mirrored in Barbara's emotional attachment at this time to a woman who had been her classmate, her companion in establishing summer stock theater in Bennington town, and never her lover. Emily Sweetser is the "nimble evader/ running softly at my words." The poems of this year are poignant and as much about the search for a role for herself in the world, a search for subjects for her poetry, as they are about Emily. This was the year that twenty-two year old Barbara was living on Morton Street in New York, trying to support herself with part time odd jobs in the theater, and writing—or attempting—poetry.

The poems of this section and the next, the ones about her winter on South Mountain Road and life with her family, are frequently self-doubting. She doesn't know her own direction, nor can she see what her "proper" subject for poetry ought to be. "I am the bewildered bombed limb alighted across the/ street from its body," she wrote of her disorientation. Perhaps she meant she was separated from Emily, but I think her real concern was to take control of her life. "I have been rigged and launched," she said, "so/ I must be a boat." If so, her plea was not to be "a paper boat sailed down the drain." Similarly, she worried that she had lost control when the car she was driving went into a skid and nearly slammed into the rocks.

Her letters from that period reveal the details behind the imagery. She and Emily quarreled desperately and frequently about their relationship, about their work together at Bennington, and about Barbara's proposal of marriage to Emily's brother, John Sweetser.[27]

Much of her life seemed as out of her control as that car on the icy road. During this time in her life, when she was looking for something she couldn't name and couldn't find, Barbara joined the Episcopalian Church. In a letter to her father explaining that step, she insisted she did not join out of any desire to escape.

> The church doesn't mean sweetness and light to me at all....I did not think to save myself from anything by joining. I tossed and tossed a bit before taking the step just because it meant to me the assumption of a responsibility and a real discipline, and meant agreeing not to dodge anything, but to accept always what life should happen to give me, meant working steadily for the strength to reject nothing or no one, trying, laboring to spot the distortion of good in people, and fighting this.[28]

Discipline, the need to take control, not to dodge—these traits she was consciously developing would serve Barbara well in her later life as a political activist. It is also easy to understand, in this context, that her attraction to the church and her attraction to political activism both shared a dynamic sense of community and belonging. The search for a community was lifelong for Barbara, Vida remembers. "She had a terrible need to belong to things. It's why she worked in the theater for a while. There was a family, always in every production....And the church provided, in a way, the same kind of thing."[29]

Barbara's friend of her later life, fellow activist and community member, Blue Lunden, felt that Barbara was drawn, not so much to groups, but to "like-minded people. Her desire was to be loving in all of her relationships, to create the Beloved Community," a community of awareness and consciousness. Her description of what she expects in joining the Episcopalian Church—to labor "to spot the distortion of good in people"—seems very similar to her later insistence on that kind of loving attention in the feminist communities in which she found herself, the communities she began to try and create.

* * *

"When she was at college, she was this radiant, beautiful creature. Everybody resonated to this. She was utterly beautiful. I remember being dazzled the first time I met her. It was probably my first day there."[30] Vida Ginsberg was a freshman at Bennington during Barbara's senior year. During that year and the summer that followed, they were co-workers in the theater group. Barbara's younger brother

Chip, Quentin Deming, came over from Dartmouth to join the stock company. Vida remembers being in love with both of them, in a way, but she was reluctant to take on "emotional tethering" of any kind. It was the summer of 1940, when they were both on the Bennington summer school faculty, that Barbara and Vida's relationship became more involved.[31]

The assumptions of this relationship do not match, however, some more contemporary notions of a partnership and do need to be made explicit. Even when Vida and Barbara were living together, and they mostly lived apart during their relationship, it was assumed that they would have other lovers, that either or both would date men. Vida was always aware of her feelings for Chip. She saw herself as Barbara's confidant and, sometimes, as her rescuer. Barbara saw men socially and had several sexual encounters with women, including the wife of a fellow student at Case Western Reserve and Lotte Lenya while she was working in New York theater. In her journals, Barbara records that the woman at Case Western Reserve saw their affair as "no threat to [her] marriage." The others? "Fell in love, or became infatuated, a few times. How many? Lenya? Very briefly, Liana. Irma."[32] And at the same time she carried around a scrap of paper in her wallet on which she had scribbled a note for a letter she wrote to Vida in the early 1940s (Barbara kept a copy of nearly every word she ever wrote), addressed to "Most dear most near girl," remembering "what weight your body was, what wind and what murmur your breath was, and the kiss it was in my mouth, and how your fingers woke me, and what a springtime lay upon me. I love you."[33]

The explicitness of Barbara's letters to Vida during these years are in marked contrast to what she felt able to write in her poetry. Concealing the subject, she writes of birds and green imagery and "noon...is a flood/ that bears us upon its breast," rather than herself feeling Vida's weight on her breast.

Barbara, the poet, becomes a figure in a Persian miniature "praying in a thicket" or a traveler in a Japanese Noh play waiting "to meet...the appropriate ghosts." Somehow, the passion is lost in the transition into what Barbara could accept as poetic image.

For nothing in these poems approaches the richness and nervous trajectory of the letters between 1939 and July of 1949 when Vida married Barbara's brother Chip. One scrap of Barbara's writing to Vida insists, "you are my wife (if you will be)…I love you." Another agrees, "yes, you suffocate me. The answer, faithfully, is yes, you do. It is I, though, who bury my head." When they are apart, Barbara writes, "I miss our life together. I hope for it to begin again. And would hope beyond that (if life were simple). I kiss your mouth until you ask for breath." During the infatuation with Lenya, Barbara sends Vida her love letter to Lenya— hoping, she says, to break the infatuation. And she writes to Lenya,

> your kisses crowd in upon me, your tongue is between my lips, to silence me. But it is true. I cannot. When I told Vida of you, she, so to speak, granted me a divorce. But I cannot divorce her. Until she takes a husband or I take a husband, I am pledged to her. [34]

When Vida left New York in 1947 to work at the Salzburg Seminar in Austria with F.O. Matthessen, Margaret Mead, and others, she felt fairly sure her role as Barbara's lover had come to an end. Barbara, however, was working on the apartment on 19th Street in New York where she meant for her and Vida to live. Wallpaper samples accompanied her letters to Europe, as did questions about how they would arrange their lives: "If your decision is to marry Chip, will you wish to live at home until it happens, or with me?" But the letter ended far less dispassionately:

> But I dream strange dreams of you at night. A stranger is in my arms, and I outraged and miserable and protesting, and then suddenly the stranger says something to me gently and I recognize her to be you! and fainting in astonishment and in relief and in love, I sink on your breast.[35]

A day later, Barbara celebrated her thirtieth birthday and wrote, "Being, then, thirty years old and of adult mind, I write to say to you that I love you, not lightly but soberly and with all my being, and very soberly desire to be married to you for all my days." But within a year, Vida married Chip.

The assurances of mutual love were there—among the three of them. Barbara lived with Vida and Chip in their new home in California for a while, but the poetry reflects, in a typically hidden way, the tug of war between her intentions—openness, love, sharing—and her emotional reality—"Fie, the worm is in my branches again." The last three poems in this section show her alone and wandering. She may "set my crooked step to be caught," but there was no one to snare her. She could wander midnight streets, but she lay in her bed alone. And she has realized that love, the image of green in so many of the early poems, "can be torn from the breast."

Wounded, working desperately to be reconciled emotionally to the two people she was closest to in the world at this time, it would seem from notes she left that Barbara had a brief re-encounter with Norma Millay, but while the "Retrospective" was comforting, that relationship could never create the home, the community of like-minded, loving people she sought. Barbara, hoping perhaps that distance would best help this process, left for Europe. She was able to live on a small legacy left to her by her Aunt Eleanor, her father Harold's only unmarried sister, a woman who had supported herself as a single woman throughout her life and who was Barbara's staunch supporter in the family.[36] Barbara also wanted to commit herself in new and significant ways to her writing.

The poems in the section "Annie" are from this period. Annie is Anne Poor, Bessie Breuer's daughter, the young woman with whom Barbara was virtually raised. Anne Poor had tried Bennington for a year and left. She served in the Army as a War Artist during World War II. She and Barbara saw each other intermittently, usually when Barbara was visiting Bessie, sometimes on family vacations to Florida or Cuba. Anne was a painter like her stepfather, Henry Poor, not a writer like her mother. The Poors were never wealthy, and in her early thirties Anne escaped to Anticoli, Italy, for a while—where she could live very, very cheaply and paint. Annie remembers that they both worked during that summer, that Barbara "kept her schedule. She lived in a small hotel….She was Spartan."[37]

Barbara told the story of this time in Europe in her novel, *A Humming Under My Feet*.[38] She began the book, as she said in the Introduction, in 1952, working from the journals she kept. Several of the poems in this section were written during that experience and appear in the novel. They are love poems, but they are also the poems of a thirty-five year old woman who has been turned loose from all that is familiar to her. In these poems, she was asking her childhood friend to be her lover. She was pursuing a woman who loved her as a friend, and did not want to be her lover. In these poems, the Big Dipper itself was "up-ended/ in a question mark." Barbara's question was about how to love ("If I love her lightly now"), but it was also about how to survive loving deeply and passionately without becoming love's victim ("Then I am love's, and not love mine"). The questions were not to be answered for many years.

In the 1950s Barbara's writing was beginning to be published more regularly. Poems appeared intermittently in small journals. In 1953 *The New Yorker* published "A Giro;" in 1954 *Charm* magazine published "Death and the Old Woman," two of the stories in the later collection, *Wash Us and Comb Us*. She was writing film reviews for several journals. And in 1954, during a visit to Bessie Breuer's house, Barbara met a painter friend of Anne Poor's—Mary Meigs. The second or third time they were together, Barbara took Mary to look at an apartment in New York she was thinking of renting. Mary remembers "looking out the window and saying, 'Would you like to live with me in my house in Wellfleet?' And Barbara was utterly amazed at my proposing."[39] They remained together for fifteen years.

It was also in 1954 that Barbara's father died. "My life changed very much at this time," Barbara wrote. "I began to live, and then lived for many years, with a woman who knew that she chose to be a lesbian."[40] She was thirty-seven.

Barbara and Mary's early life together shifted between the (unheated) house in Wellfleet and winters in New York. They socialized in Wellfleet with neighbors like Edmund Wilson and his wife Elena, Mary McCarthy and her husband Bowden Broadwater. Both worked in the house. Mary Meigs recalls that:

> We had very serious schedules. I guess I got up earlier and started working on my painting in my studio. Bobbie worked in the morning, but mostly in the afternoons. We did not share in the household things and the cooking. I did the bigger portion of it. She did behave like a man, as far as I was concerned, in the sense that she was completely immersed in her work. She worked very slowly.[41]

In her poems of the mid fifties, Barbara is writing about this relationship as a marriage, but she is not using explicit pronouns. "Our arms drew a circle/ in which we lay," could be about any pair of lovers; and the reference to the flood and the ark seems deliberately misleading, since the animals who went "two of a kind aboard" were male and female.

Within a few years, however, the poems are "locked in winter," and the reader remembers that Barbara's image of love was the color green. In "Three Prayers" she asks, "can/ A man/ Wear green a second time?" She wanted it to be true, but her heart told her it wasn't. Mary Meigs has written extensively about the difficulties of this relationship in her own book, *Lily Briscoe: A Self-Portrait*.[42]

The poems indicate that Barbara felt Mary's withdrawal, but they do not tell us exactly why, at this time in her life, Barbara began to be drawn to political activism. In 1959 she and Mary took a long trip around the world that began in Japan, took them to India where Barbara began reading the works of Gandhi, and brought them back via Tel Aviv where she met with Martin Buber. The following spring, while Barbara was vacationing in Cuba with the Poors, she managed an informal meeting with Castro, only a short time after his triumphant march into Havana. When she returned to the U.S., an article about Cuba began her public identification with politics. By the end of the 1960s, she was an active member of the Committee for Nonviolent Action, taking part in demonstrations, marches, and civil disobedience. Mary watched this transformation, not happy with it, but unable to stop it. "I was in mourning," she recalls. "I thought her new metamorphosis prevented her from being an artist anymore. She actually stopped working on her stories."

Barbara's withdrawal, the redirection of her attention away from the relationship, changed their life. Neither woman expected Mary's response to Barbara's political involvement—that she would feel threatened as an artist, that she would feel guilty about being an artist because that cut her off from "real life." Within two years, Mary had fallen in love with another artist, Canadian writer Marie-Claire Blais, and once again Barbara found herself involved in a triangular relationship. For six years, these three powerful women tried to make a love triangle work. Sometimes it did. Mary has happy memories of a house in Maine, their "lovely little house in the middle of the fields and woods. We'd go out at sunset with the dog.... I remember being happy there." But the tensions inevitably returned.[43] Basically a peacemaker, Barbara tried to make the triangle a peaceful one. In a letter to Marie Claire she promised,

> I won't harden myself. And most nights I will simply look in the door and say "Goodnight"; but some nights I'll lie next to you and we'll talk; and that is a coming together, in itself—to give each other the truth of ourselves. So we'll see how life goes. Just don't be afraid of me ever— afraid, I mean, to let me know where you are. For we really are friends, deeply. (And—it has to be the truth that one lives.)[44]

During these years, Barbara left more and more frequently. A typical year's chronology which Barbara kept for her own information included, to use 1965 as an example, "Jan. 7—Began abdomen exercises from book....Jan. 29—mailed Part V....Feb. 22—Malcolm X assassinated!....Feb. 23—now on editorial board LIB....Feb. 25—letter fm Bob O. abt movie book, poems etc....March 12—M's opening."[45] The opening of a show of Mary Meigs' painting seems from this distance to be a very small item on Barbara's list. Barbara traveled up and down the east coast, flew to Paris, and in April of 1966 she flew to North Vietnam. Home must have seemed further and further away. There are no poems that record these years.

In the personal chronology for 1967 is a single note for May 22. "To Verlaines. J drove me Columbia." Verlaines are Oscar and Jane Verlaine. Jane had been a student, briefly, at Bennington College also. She remembered meeting Barbara there, but she was awed by her and never presumed they could be friends. Years later, her marriage basically ended, Jane Verlaine met Barbara again. They visited. In 1968 Jane separated from Oscar, and by 1969 she and her two children were living with Barbara. Jane's account of this courtship is the subject of her book, *Something Not Yet Ended*,[46] which was published in 1981 while Jane and Barbara were living in their home in Sugarloaf Key, Florida. Barbara's first account of this relationship is in her poetry: "Each night I cling to you—/ A floating spar." She wonders if they are drifting toward home or out to sea, wonders if they are, instead, struggling toward a new land. She has visions of a new life as "life as it has been drowns."

Getting to shore in her new life with Jane was not easy. Barbara's life was very full and busy—and very public. She was writing and publishing continually. She was involved in political actions, political discussions and events. She looked at every issue as it arose. Disarmament. Civil Rights. Feminism. And finally, with Jane, she must confront her own oppression as a lesbian, because Jane's ex-husband threatened a custody suit, naming Barbara as the reason Jane was unfit to raise her own children. In a letter to Dave Dellinger, she described how Oscar told Jane "right in front of the kids" that he "forbids them to have any more contact with her Bull Dike [sic] friend." Not sure how far Oscar wanted to take his anger, quite sure how unfavorably the courts would look at lesbian mothers in 1969, both women were aware that Jane might have to give up "her plan to share a house with me. And then we will simply wait, until the kids are older, to make our lives together. And call this a war-time separation."[47] Dave Dellinger, at this time, had his own legal concerns to worry about and asked Barbara to write a piece about the issues involved in the trial of the Chicago Seven. But she was unable to take it on, exhausted by the emotional strain of the custody case and the happier exhaustion of working with Jane on the old farm house in Monticello, New York, where they were finally able to move with Jane's two children.

During this period, Barbara experienced a growing separation from the anti-war, nonviolence movement. Letters from friends accused her of dropping out of the movement; Barbara explained over and over again that in fighting her way toward the right to live with the person she loved, she was not leaving the movement, but expanding it. Ray Robinson, a black comrade on southern Peace Walk through Albany, Georgia, in the early sixties, complained, "Well if you have never been to the bottom, complete bottom, no you cannot understand me. I can never forget the struggle."[48]

"I lie at the bottom of my spirit's well," Barbara wrote of that difficult year, answering Robinson's complaint in a poem. The custody case, Dellinger's trial—she can't seem to separate life and death; and yet the poem represents, I believe, Barbara reclaiming her life and her voice. She is writing in the first person again, writing with less and less concealment, writing with passion about the things that concern her, as she comes to terms with life in the open.

"When I decided to come out publicly as a lesbian," she said in an interview for the journal *Kalliope*, "I prepared myself for this step by writing the poem which begins, 'Behind her the sea hisses.' Or rather, I could say that the writing of the poem was the taking of this step."[49]

In the poem, Barbara "means to dance away my fear/...And dare be naked, known/ As whatever self I am." It was a good intention for her to hold in those volatile earlier days of feminism, when to be public as a lesbian was to be sometimes accused of destroying feminism, sometimes accused of not doing enough to help the lesbian cause.[50] In 1971 Barbara was on her way to deliver a talk at the War Resisters' League national conference in Athens, Georgia. Her talk was to be about anger,[51] anger in general and her newly-discovered, very personal anger at the man who had tried to dominate her, Jane's ex-husband. Enroute, her car was in a serious accident. Barbara, who had been asleep in the back seat, barely survived; both lungs were collapsed, her pelvis and both legs broken. She was in a body cast for nearly a year; her body never recovered fully from the trauma.

Her spirit, her will to learn and explore, her passion for life—these seemed undiminished. In response to Barbara's need for a warm climate, she and Jane moved to Sugarloaf Key, Florida, in what might have seemed a retreat from the world. But neither meant to retreat; both continued to work with women, with lesbians for the issues that compelled them. Gradually, the feminist and lesbian feminist world discovered Barbara. She was not hard to find, even tucked away on Sugarloaf Key, because her writing and publishing were more prolific than at any other time in her life. *We Cannot Live Without Our Lives* appeared in 1974, *Remembering Who We Are* was self-published in 1981, and *We Are All Part of One Another: A Barbara Deming Reader* came out in 1984, just before Barbara's death. Two other books, *Prisons That Could Not Hold*, which contained her earlier *Prison Notes* and her new writing about the Seneca Women's Peace Encampment, and her novel, *A Humming Under my Feet*, were published after her death.

Her writing at this time was nourished by a growing women's

community. Barbara's political theory, her writing, had never been a purely cerebral act. She always struggled to make the theoretical real in her life, walking through the segregated south in an integrated group, standing in Hanoi during the very real and devastating bombings. On Sugarloaf, she and Jane became members of a feminist community. They demonstrated against violence and pornography in films, they gave support to a shelter for battered women; and their personal home grew gradually to accommodate others who became their family, part of their own beloved community.

The last poems in this volume are about death. Two were written to her mother when Katherine experienced a health crisis.

Barbara did not know her mother would outlive her by two years; nor could she have known, consciously, that she was addressing herself in the admonishment—"Death stands near...but don't fear it.\ It waits to lay on you a friendly hand." She did know that the act, the struggle, to write poems...

> had found for me the psychic balance that I needed. There's a special sense in which I would call poetry supremely useful. So much of what we need to know we need to know not just with our minds but with our very bodies. Since poetry speaks in rhythms, in music, our very bodies are able to absorb its messages. Some of these messages our intellects by themselves could not even quite say what they are. Yet they can be necessary life messages.[52]

It is fitting that Barbara Deming's last poem was a poem of her body, a poem in which the body chanted her grunts and groans as Barbara worked her way toward death and change.

Before her death, Barbara spoke to each of the women named in this volume of poetry who were still living—Emmie, Vida, Annie, Mary, and Jane. Vida, Mary, and Jane were all present in Barbara's final days, and Mary, Jane, and the members of Barbara's beloved community were with her until her death. Blue Lunden describes Barbara's death as "one of her rewards for working to build beloved community," an extraordinary and loving series of circles, rituals, dances, and sharing.[53]

Barbara Deming died at her home on Sugarloaf Key on August 2, 1984, leaving a legacy of how to be in the world. Her poetry is only a small part of that legacy, rather than the major expression she had hoped for it. And yet we read her poetry for the lessons it contains—not always the lessons she had intended—and for the important questions her work suggests.

When I first began sorting through the files and boxes that consisted of Barbara Deming's literary estate, I was struck by some of the early poems I found, most around 1934 or 1935. They were the vibrant, exuberant poems of Barbara's first love affair. But I saw in the upper corner of several of these early poems, written in Barbara's handwriting, the word "omit." These must have been some of the poems she showed to her first college advisor, the kind of poems that Genevieve Taggard didn't like. I don't know when the word "omit" was written on those pages, but when Barbara compiled this group of poems just before her death, she reinserted several of those poems that had been omitted for so many years. I have added several others that I found in her files, her journals, poems I presume she would have wanted to use if she had remembered them. [54] These poems are part of our heritage, and the word "omit" is our heritage also.

When I let these poems speak to me, they are asking questions. They want to know what risks I am not willing to take because I think the cost will be too high. They ask if I really understand the cost of not taking the risk. They speak to me every time I think that some feeling or political thought or action might not be suitable subjects for poetry. They ask me, Isn't passion what creates poetry? Do you need to find a safe subject? A suitably artistic subject?

"Now I have tasted of the wind's wild draught," wrote the seventeen year old high school student. "How can I tear away my lips, wind-yearning?" Barbara Deming knew about passion. She really did. I am glad the record of her wind-yearning is here for us to study.

END NOTES

(1)Notes on poems, September 27, 1982.

(2)Interview with James Merrill, Stonington, CT, July 12, 1994.

(3)"The Transgress," in The Speed of Darkness, 1968.

(4)Interview with Mary Meigs, January 16, 1992.

(5)Notes on poems, September 27, 1982.

(6)Interview with Quentin Deming, July 11, 1992.

(7)"South Mountain Road," p 63.

(8)Letter to Harold Deming, undated.

(9)Letter to Harold Deming, late summer, 1940.

(10)Interview with Angus Deming, October 26, 1992.

(11)Letter to Barbara Deming, April 15, 1941.

(12)Notes for a resume, around 1941.

(13)Resume, 1946.

(14)Letter to Katherine Deming, March 7, 1934.

(15)e.e. cummings, "[If i have made, my lady, intricate]," 1926.

(16)Letter to Katherine Deming, March, 1934.

(17)Interview with Anne Poor, March 17, 1992.

(18)Resume, Positions Held, 1946.

(19)"South Mountain Road," p 63.

(20)Interviews with MacDonald (July 8, 1992), Quentin (July 11, 1992), and Angus Deming (October 26, 1992).

(21)Interview with Vida Ginsberg Deming, March 4, 1992.

(22)Letter to Katherine Deming, September 7,1934.

(23)Interview with Vida Deming, May 1, 1995.

(24)Journal copy of a letter to Dorothy Case, 1937-8.

(25)Barbara omitted this poem from the manuscript she compiled at the end of her life, but it was not clear to me whether that choice was deliberate, or whether she had merely lost track of this poem in her files.

(26)Letter from Anne Poor, July 24, 1995.

(27)Undated letter (circa 1940) from Barbara Deming to John Sweetser: "Saturday night, after telling me that you were not in love with me, you added: 'Good God, I don't know you' And you of course do not; and I do not know you."

(28)Letter to Harold Deming, late summer, 1940.

(29)Interview with Vida Deming, July 11, 1992.

(30)Interview with Vida Ginsberg Deming, March 4, 1992.

(31)Letter from Vida Deming, July 30, 1995.

(32)Notes to Poems, September 27, 1982.

(33)Letters between Barbara and Vida during the 1940s.

(34)Letter to Lotte Lenya, December 1944 January 1945.

(35)Letter to Vida Ginsberg, July 22, 1947.

(36)Letter from Anne Poor, July 24, 1995.

(37)Interview with Anne Poor, March 17, 1992.

(38)Published by The Women's Press, Limited: London, England, 1985.

(39)Interview with Mary Meigs, January 16, 1992.

(40)Notes about the poems taken from comments Barbara wanted to make during a reading. Undated.

(41)Interview with Mary Meigs, January 16, 1992.

(42)Published by Talonbooks, Vancouver, 1981.

(43)Interview with Mary Meigs, January 18, 1992.

(44)Letter to Marie Claire Blais, undated.

(45)Barbara Deming's personal chronology, notes, 1958-1968.

(46) Jane Gapen [Verlaine], Something Not Yet Ended, Pagoda Publications, 1981. Distributed by Naiad Press:Tallahassee, FL.

(47)Letter to Dave Dellinger, August 30, 1969.

(48)"Confronting One's Own Oppression," in We Cannot Live Without Our Lives, (Grossman Publishers, 1974), p. 119.

(49)"An Interview with Barbara Deming," by Ruthann Robson, in Kalliope (Florida Junior College at Jacksonville). Vol. 6 No.1, 1984

(50)In a letter written December 1, 1972, to Rita Mae Brown, for example, Barbara explains about the custody case and why she could not, for some years, be more public as a lesbian. She is answering Rita Mae Brown's question and challenge: "Were you willing to take risks, deprivation, pain, for the sake of peace and Black people—will you do it for yourself and for me and other Lesbians/women? I think until you do I will think of you as a kind of Lady Bountiful bestowing your energies and passions on the other oppressed and sidestepping your own oppression and that of other Lesbians. Its the most dangerous one to face, I can't really blame you but until you do face it, I can't really trust you."

(51)"On Anger," in We Cannot Live Without Our Lives (New York: Grossman Publishers, 1974), p. 36-51. This book is dedicated "to my lesbian sisters."

(52)Kalliope, p. 39.

(53)Conversation with Blue Lunden, August 14, 1995.

(54)Poems added to the Norma section include "she held the flower," "angel," "Lady, some pain," "To E.S.M.," and "Meeting."

Wind Madness
1933

Friend's Academy Prize

Now I have tasted of the wind's wild draught
And felt its hot wine in my blood mad-burning,
Till I have drunk the last fierce dregs
How can I tear away my lips, wind-yearning?

Now I have raced with the wind that once,
Flushed with the passion of the evening sky,
Swept by the frenzy of dry leaves wild-whirling,
Shouting against the wind's great cry,

How can I go on living, bearing
A city's shrieking pain,
Aching with noise and hoarse with
Screaming to God for the wind again?

Now I have brought away my lips
Burning, wind-passion-stained
From the deep potion,
How can I leave the cup undrained?

NORMA

1933-1934

Barbara Deming in the theater, 1930s

✿ ✿ ✿

lady

two frighteNed small birds tremble
      their wings against the walls
      of my bOdy

the tremble of their wings is pain   lady
the tremble of theiR wings is love

two frightened small birds treMble
      their wings against the walls of my body
the tremble of their wings is your nAme   lady

⑥ ⑥ ⑥

she held the flower cold up against her cheek
bones in the dark the petals flattened cold up
against her cheekbones this flower your
fingers you had danced with this flower in your
mouth your tongue had been pink like a cat's
tongue and slender touching the petals you had
danced with this flower in your mouth held in
your teeth your teeth biting the petals the
petals cold up against her cheekbones she held
the flower cold up against her cheekbones in
the dark.

⑥ ⑥ ⑥

      angel
you said   (still morning and no wind in the air)
i love you
and
          o angel
if i was silent
and had no words to say
it was because the words i needed
the words so trembling on my lips
you had that moment
suddenly
taken from me
and set quivering against my breast

❦ ❦ ❦

Lady
Some pain is beautiful

Sweet agony of black aching earth
Breathless pain of wind

Thrilling mighty agony of birth

Lady
Some pain is beautiful
Lady
I strain the singing pain of loving you
against my lips.

❦ ❦ ❦

i was content before i met you
with the sound of leaves falling
with the sound of wind
and leaves falling—

Now
though the leaves fall
the wind rises
        and the leaves fall
what are they to me
who am shaken by stronger winds?

᠖ ᠖ ᠖

I.

Ha i taunted
Flung to the winds my cry
Ha
And the sun was at my back
And i flung to the winds
    my cry
Shouldering the air
Oh i am strong
I am strong and the sun
    is at my back
    And I stood

Taunting
And my cry
Trembled against the sky
And even as i stood
    legs wide
    face against the air
I was pierced by the song
As by a shaft of light
And stood
My breath cold
The air sharp against my side
Afraid

II.

Shouldering the night
I stepped
Tight-muscled
Along the wind

I will think i said
Of other things
I will look at cliffs and the sea
And watch the flight of white sea-birds
Nor think any more of her

I watched the sea whiten against the cliffs
And flash sun against the wings
    of the white sea-birds
I tried to forget her
But always the white cliffs
    pressed to the sea
And always
    the sea-birds kissed with their wings
    the sea-splashed light
And the crying of their throats ached in my wrists
And i knew i could not forget

✿ ✿ ✿

the leaves of the tree made darkness patterns
against the sky
and sunlight patterns
upon the earth

we did not speak

but singing was stretched thin between our finger
tips

✿ ✿ ✿

I had leaned always to the wind and thought me lover
of the stars
but tonight
there is no wind up and no stars
and
I am desiring oh so your breasts

I had thought it was the wind sung in me
Tonight there is no wind
I had thought it was the stars burned in me
and no stars
and here is this burning and this singing in me.

๑ ๑ ๑

o to be sunlight thrust
to your body
shivering One with you
to be shivering sunlight-thrust to you
ohgodbeloved

๑ ๑ ๑

wet earth to my lips
i sing
o and to touch her breasts with gentle fingers
o and to touch
    slant-fingered
    o
    and to touch slant-thrill-fingered
    her warm breasts

i weep to o wet earth and my fingers
where my fingers sing
ohgodohgodohgodohgodohgodohgod

ᰔ ᰔ ᰔ

through rain went
and what is the rain
you said

thin singing in my side
it was

through mist
and what is the mist

rain there was
and mist
and
as
i lean
to the lightning of your body
what is this white tree ribbed to the night

୭ ୭ ୭

i set my heels criss-slant climbing of black straight rock
fingerly crevice stretched wrist to vein of rock to vein
ankle to sharp wind-crying light
stood
at length
column to the sun
darling
and with the white slender singing of you in my side
wept.

୭ ୭ ୭

It is not that there is a lack of seeing you
)in the small crazy fists of children running
          always
          in the sweet proud throats
          always
          in the brave sad mouths of women(
buT

when i shout to the children they do not turn
and
women have a way of seeing past me so out at their
          gardens in the sun

Dedication

Kneeling
they offer her each one
      his soul   done in a

      package taut

(each one)
      with the lean-twisted
cord of pain.

Let it be said of her that she always puts away paper bags
folded
in a drawer.

To E.S.M.

I would not wish to meet you
Or have you meet me—
I would prefer you did not even rise,
upon my entrance, from your chair.
This is all I ask:
That I might sit and watch you once
Whom I have watched
So often in my dreams
That you are part of me.

I would not wish to talk
Or have you talk to me.
I would prefer that when I came
into the room, you should not even know.
This is all I ask:
That I might sit and watch you once—
And then might go.

Meeting

I had heard so much about you,
Waited with such breathlessness for you to come,
Through time seared with the agony of waiting.

And then you came—
You came—we shook hands—and you said:
"It's nice to meet you"—and you said:
"I'm afraid I'm frightfully late."

I had dreamed so much about your coming,
Waited achingly
Through time arched with the agony of dreaming.

And then you came—
You came—we talked of mother-in-laws
And income taxes,
We talked about the new play at the Guild.
"I think it's going to have a run," you said.
I said: "It looks that way."

I had prayed so much about your coming,
Prayed unceasingly
Through time white with the agony of praying.

And then you came—
You came—we talked—you said goodbye.
You said: "Do look me up when you're in town."
And then you went.

CASEY

1934-1938

Barbara Deming,
Bennington College, 1935

❦ ❦ ❦

the rain is my lover
          my body
          i break open to the heart of me
          crying to the rain
          touch me
          touch me
i break open my body that the rain may get inside of me
stretched
          to my hunger   cool
          cool   be in my narrow limbs
          its wrists
          are up in my wrists   and its thighs
          pressed
          down
          in
          my thighs   the blade of it
          along
          my
          muscles
          and its tongue cool
          cool   in my head
the rain stretches
up
inside of me   ever so cool and
giddy
through me
and
ever so strong   singing
against my sides   the rain
          is my lover whom i lie waiting   with
          my body broken
          open
and it will come
and with fingers cool as rubbed stone
touch
my naked heart

❦ ❦ ❦

My heart
at this invasion
is solemn.
As flowers relinquish night incredulous
my heart suffers your persuasion.
Morning collapses each flower tinily
as cat would with tapping paw.
My heart can fashion no evasion.

❦ ❦ ❦

my wings unfolded
from the rocking sweetness of you
alone now
i ride the waves

sea-move flat to my sides
is gentle—
carries my leaning body

i make a child of my longing for you
and cradle it
meek in my breast with tiny
crooning

❧ ❧ ❧

Her hide from such dancing was as sleek with water as
the pool

     The pool was so shell-black it took no shadow
nor even the reflection of her two eyes over it   lit
with desire

     But at her dancing one day the birds   (from the
branches)   dropped suddenly leaving in their shape the
sky   and the pool where their reflections fell skidded
with light

     Watching on the pool's surface their intricate
legs   stagger she was filled with jealousy
       and with her body broke the pool
       the reflections like narrow fish in panic
fleeing

there is this awareness of pain
stretched to my muscles
and these my knuckles to the stinging pits of my eyes
        (and there a bird lifts
        laughing with crazy throat)
and there is this awareness of pain
stamped to the hollow of my breath
and
        if i lean clenched questions to a lifting bird
        with crazy laughing throat
        will it perhaps answer me
for
i cannot quite remember what it is
i weep

I have taken my heart out tinily
to contemplate.
It leaps in my fist
pulse shrill
thrilling my fingers,
leaping in its tiny coat.
Pressed again into my narrow side
the beat of it still frightens
my fingers.

"*Cats love eyes*" Yeats

Listen
cats love eyes
they move tinily on leaning paws
stride slanting up the whole body
as movement tightened along a whip snapped
hence my preoccupation

this man's gesture
completing immediate object
culminates
stride at the hip
movement of arm for lifting
stiffening off at shoulder
to stop there

i am seeking a lover who can move like a cat
with taut stretchiness
swift almost unmotion
animal move

The house
Is not the man's
He moves
In it
Like a skater who puts on shoes now
And tries to walk
Comes downstairs expecting a last step
Where there is none.

The tree
Was felled last night
But birds still
Hang in the branchless air
Silent
And tread water.

House tree man bird
Has the dramatist erred?

Bird man house tree
Can the actors not agree?

Tree bird house man
Had they better give up the plan

And—man bird tree house—
Take their bows?

❦ ❦ ❦

This
is a bird in the hand:
feathers small
and the weak claws under it,
beak and eyelids sillied with the extravagant
batting, opening and closing, peck of a child's fan. This
is your sleeping beauty: hack
through the jungle and
come on her
cold as a cat on a slab,
the lips pouted these one hundred years for your lips.

this bird is drunk
beaked to rib of cloud
wind in her eyes
she weeps in her craziness
drops
beak drinking wind
quill-shivering—

a line from here to here

Merrygoround

Here
one evening
we circled bemused—
the painted horses rising and falling,
stare slick and sorry,
the wooden lids raised from the eyes like a child's
and the ears stiff,
hooves stiff,
high slick buttocks rising and falling in the vaporous mirrors
to a glib calliope.
Here
you circled on your painted mount
found and lost to me,
betrayed to me
at your ease.

The Taunt

Crazed with the slendered ecstasy of pain
I turned and fled her
With the bitter-arrowed taunt of her laughter
Fled her
Blading my body to the wind
Mad with the coppery wound
Of a flight
Of birds
Across a slim mouth
Ran
Blind with the trembling hurt
Turned and fled her
Stamping laughter into the earth
With lean hard heels

Tragedian

1.
Her parasol
in the garden
where other ladies also drift
is dog utterance
of an identity.
Under the long boughs
she wavers
mouthing a sorrow
with ferocity;
waits for evening to pale suddenly about her,
bell strike
or clock gesture;
waits for a wind to shake a rain of worms
from the long boughs
to fall like small bloom
with silk tap
on her parasol;
walks in a silly hurricane of grief
leering sidewise at the other
thieves
in the garden.

2.
Monday
her grief (like dust)
is shaken in the air to mark
departure.
Tuesday grief's her child
bullied
with dogged
lullaby.
Wednesday
grief is a
goldfish
circling for the infatuate eye
under glass.

Under the floor
Rat moves
Under the grass
Mole.
The wind
Has its teeth in leaves and in clouds and
Won't hush.
Neither will the brook,
Its teeth full of pebbles,
Be still.

Have you ever at night when there was a
fire built seen flame reflected in the window
and the flame through the glass burn in a
quince tree or a flower bed or a cloud and the
flame wave cheerily but the branch not ignited
nor flower bed blackened nor cloud become vapor?
I dread to awaken some day and find my powers
no more real than this flame which does not eat
but ornaments the bush, lapping away stilly.

EMMIE

1938-1940

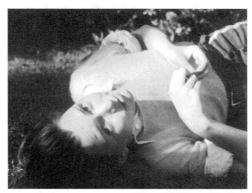

Photo by Roger Burling
Barbara Deming, 1936

✻ ✻ ✻

nimble evader
running softly at my words
frail animal
scared and infuriating
beautiful as Nefertiti

evasive as swimmer under water

✻ ✻ ✻

you elude my arms
like water
and my mouth

like smoke

✻ ✻ ✻

Your star
sighs,
heaves—
turns from my
ponderous love,
casts its beacon
into another region,
your star which
whitens the air,
turns from my love
like a buoy sliding through the waters.

＊ ＊ ＊

swimmer in a lake
can encounter sudden currents
of colder water
I never know when
I'll encounter the shock of
remembering you

＊ ＊ ＊

I heard a great dog lapping behind me.
It was a train and ran over me.
I heard a great train panting behind me.
It was a dog and ate me up.

＊ ＊ ＊

I stare out into the street
at nightfall.
Window panes are blue,
the ladders of fire escapes ashen.
Parked cars look like bleached fish skeletons.
Kids are burning Christmas trees and wreaths in the gutters.
They stand about and gaze
as sailors on shore would gaze at ships burning
at sea—
the ships blazing and fading.
The exploding sounds and scents of these fires
hold me rapt, too.

❋ *❋* *❋*

This cat—this apparition—visits by way of
my window, smells badly, has been where?
Has the charms of a sailor.
When I was hunting for this room to rent, I was shown into
many rooms, still inhabited, each its peculiar aura,
its attempt at life. This cat probably enters all of
those rooms, and more; its fur rubs each, takes something
with it from each.
Suddenly seeing it when I open my door is
disturbing as a ship is disturbing—spotted standing
stiff and minute on the horizon—stirs in me desire and
a sense of my isolation. So I talk to it eagerly;
stroke it and caress it fervently. And bitterly.
Or I pick it up and set it bristling in the hall.
Today I looked up from writing and saw it standing hard
and scornful in the window, and I yelled at it;
and it dropped off the sill.
The very first time I opened my door and saw it, it was lying
planted on my bed. Outrageous cat.

❋ *❋* *❋*

   This dog and its itch, its puzzled urgent
nose, never still—the itch just beyond its
reach—its whole face wrinkled back to its
skull—this flea, this torment, this
me.

   The day itself seems untroubled; it sleeps
in the teeth of my impatience. The tent of
the night is raised above me, itching not even
with stars. But beneath it this dog, with
clicking sad teeth—this flea, this me.

❈ ❈ ❈

I dreamt:
I am
coming downstairs carrying a baby.
Balance all off.
Hang onto railings.
Inch down one step at a time.
The baby shifts, its head lolling.
I sit
and try to inch down that way.

At the foot of the stairs
all the family waits
watching me

❈ ❈ ❈

I am the bewildered bombed limb alighted across the
street from its body
I am the face swollen with ivy, which in the mirror
does not recognize itself
I am the plugging inch worm which incessantly climbs
the hand which keeps replacing itself with the other hand—
inching, inching.

I tune my ear to each coming and going scuff
on the pavement
   Or yelling bell of the telephone. The yell
may be in the next half second, so I can't be at
ease. The parrot is at my neck, its beak always
in my hair.
   And out in the city I am pestered with each
particular neon blink—as in those painful candid
shots in which each bead of sweat is popping, and
the network of skin is plain
   Every sound and every smell and every particular
sight is isolate, glaring as mica. Glaring as for
one coming out of ether.
   And it might be a signal, it might be a warning.
   I count each shrill second.
   Back in my room again, fever of steam heat.
My head is knocking.
   I tune my ear to each coming and going scuff on
the pavement.

                    ❋ ❋ ❋

climb the staircase and with stupendous effort sit
and write "the little duck ate a berry"

and that not frivolously but really seeing in that
a victory of a sort
of a sort

but

i do not believe that a monkey at a typewriter in time
produces a poem

at which collapses baloonish the room about me

✳ ✳ ✳

Their very nimble bills will soon disturb
the sleek heart of the lake.
As the bills of these birds
thoughts of you will

break at my heart.

At this glass hill
so often clowned
Like horse fallen
slap on its side in a winter street
Like a landed flounder
slumped here
heavy and slack—
at love's glass hill.

✳ ✳ ✳

My unadroit love for you moves
like one making slow tracks through snow
or one who is groping through dark (here is knob,
here is railing)—
but wants of course to move
as a pebble is skipped
or as the slight blades of small spring blooms
break through the ground
neatly, lightly.

SOUTH MOUNTAIN ROAD

1939-1940

photo by Consuelo Kanaga
Barbara Deming 1945

The ascending terraces of ground, of rocky ground, now
delight my heart, the sun blaring from behind great black
shoulders of cloud, and the cold stout trees, with the stiff
buds on them, and harsh papering of leaves,
at their feet shiny run of waters, black and dogged brooks.
And sun slapping their chill upper branches, shot right up there,
tridents, forks. Stiff brush of trees at the field's end.
Yes, they bristle from the harsh cheek of this land—hair
up, fingers out. And the grasses bristle high at the knees
of the woods—like the feathers of an owl.
Yes, the beard on each hill is my delight.
And in this winter forest, the sour birds cluck and brawl,
jabber and yell. The sun rocks through
the day. Then night strips the outflung cloak of shine from
the white ground, and ice, the serpent, climbs the longest
bough to plunder buds.

❦ ❦ ❦

1.

water snake
elegant sliding body
(no elbows, no hips)
skating the wrinkled water
as through air
movement travels along its length with the tightness
and elegance of a current of
electricity.

2.

squirrel along all the branches
quicksilver running as in a tilted bowl
a disquiet along the chilly branches of this only tree
haunting every one
persistent
as the emotion
which frets
me.

✿ ✿ ✿

As I walked back from talk with my writer friend,
felt as though I could see again. Looked and saw
hillsides, trees, I had never seen before. And was
thinking would not surprise me—would not stun me,
that is—if saw to the left of me or the right of
me a monster, some new animal, or form of giant, not
reported before, sent over the mountain suddenly.
(Was thinking this because the small serpentine rock
border to the rock garden on my left, half seen out of
the corner of my left eye, could have been a large
serpent coiled there, sunning.) There is so much that
has not been seen by each of us. (To small animals this
must happen, who take things for granted just as we do.
A man walks into their neck of the woods one fine day.
Big boots of. Brings their noses up to have a look—
eyelids snapped up into the very brows.)

I have left praying until the very late at night—
already in my dreams.
I have hugged my illness about me, slumped into it,
my hands folding, my feet folding on each other.
But there is a great deal to be done.
Write of the rocks coming at me, after the car I was
driving went into that skid.
Write of my family now. At meal time. My sense of
silliness.
Write of loving E. Write of that strange wandering
through the city one day—a lost mutt. Wanted so a rug
to dream on, a fire to put my snout along. And write of
that strange apartment den in which I lived last winter.

❦ ❦ ❦

My brothers and I can sleep beyond reason, flat
on our faces, and wake stunned, drag ourselves through
the day with our faces still pressed against the glass
of sleep.

　　　We sleep as others would riot.

　　　The only way to clear ourselves is to look at this
sleep, to look at our dreams, to take our dreams into
our life.

　　　Or the days are dragged down towards the nights.

　　　For a long time I have seen myself curled in venomous
sleep. And the household stiffened around me.

　　　Plato speaks of knowledge as recollection.

　　　I must delve this sleep, this mud. Why I've been so
haunted by the shot in THE LOST WORLD of the brontosaurus,
fallen from the high plateau into mud of lava, sodden in it,
trying to pull out of it, with long long neck, with blop of
body, struggling feebly, the old vegetable eater, loose old
animal (animal a child would make in clay, dragging the
neck out too far, rolling the plump body in its hands)—
made in those days when things were brewing, were rank, the
hand of God shaping life from slime and rock.

　　　This is a dream that I keep dreaming.

　　　And all this has something to do with an entire
household. Can I possibly reconcile the family members?
Join hands with brothers?

❦❦❦

Skidding toward rocks
the wheel sitting between my hands
here I am
nothing to do but wait
quietly   seeing
just what is there
before my eyes.
The truth will make you whole.

❦❦❦

That dream I had once of breaking through ice, through
ice, through ice. Through bands. More than the
muscles can bear. And at the end, half-woke to seem
to see a severed head squatting about where my knees
were in bed.
(Hit at the wall, but my brother in the next room
didn't wake.)

❦ ❦ ❦

Remember: Descent into my parents' living room.
The lit lamp. Supper. Elbows off the table, eyes
in front! One must be a poet only in one's own
room.

❦ ❦ ❦

Oh, have been flapping shutters to, flapping shutters.
And now would toss open, bang open windows, look and
look. Have been buried alive and now would, as in the
Poe story, splinter open the box, hurl down the gate,
and stand at the door till the demon fall dead.

❦ ❦ ❦

Have been
Not admitting it all to be present, and given.
Dreaming.
If love, love. Possible or impossible because of other
person. But actual, not dreamt.
And I no more the victim of than anyone of any
love. This is not the devil. It is the devil who
says this is the devil.
Will look at everything, will not turn eyes down or
sidewise. For it is not for me to say where the hope
lies, where death is made life.

This stiff shroud of ice, this mock of bloom,
this weight, this glittering load with the appearance
of feather, is promise given of spring, this anything
but green, this load from above, most icy, most harsh,
yet there it is—spring.

❦ ❦ ❦

Night drawing in, street turning blue, my heart
shutting down. Yelling so at that ally cat who'd
come in the window. That was hatred. That old galleon
so frightened me.
And the lights of Broadway winking so. My soul
distracted, issuing at my mouth.
Climbing the subway stairs. I wrote of this:
"Climbing with curled paw the venomous flood. And
saw not Dante's four stars as he climbed out of Hell,
but ads in motion, Wrigleys sprite."
And eating each evening alone, staring, glaring into
the cold refrigerated glass of the delicatessen.
Staring at cold fatty pink sheep hung in window, its
jelly eyes.
Used to slump in movies, leaning forward to gyre and
gimble, force laughter and tears, trying to put my feet
into those slippers—blood in my shoes.
As I think in a dream to climb a flat wall and apply
self, legs and arms split out like spiders, to get up that
wall, knowing in my heart already the long fall, murder
below, the wolf, the snake, the man with knife, with gun.
The elastic-gone fall, father's arm removed, water
fathoms deep.

This is almost too much for me. I am breathing as
though I had been running.

Open the windows, open the windows, let me
look out, let these walls fall down, fall out,
let the rain in, let the birds bang in, and trees
fall in. I can't stand the steam coating these
windows, the hair falling over my eyes, the
branches across this window, the cloth hanging
on me, the smooth flesh, dim flesh, this hedge
between me and my sleeping princess—with eyes
through which I fall as through ice into the final
black water.

> My bonnie lies over the ocean
> My bonnie lies over the sea
> I love a girl who will never love me

I must undress down to the bone, take all the
pictures off the wall
        and remember who I am.

I can remember: I ran along the shore,
yawping, desolate, quite out of my mind, seeing my mother
swimming along out beyond the breakers. The breakers
between us, curling. The sea then was my father, the
masculine, the continuous rearing waves.

I sat under my mother's skirts
and wept
My father's hand was a lion's paw
and his loins
were the night
the boa constrictor who strangled the donkey in
SWISS FAMILY ROBINSON
thunder
and the elevated train on third avenue
the horse that stepped on me in the meadow,
large animal,
but who looked around at me mutely, his hoof on my foot
Yes, those were his eyes
yes, those were my cries
under my mother's skirts.

After seeing a painting by Salvador Dali

A lobster at your loins in this painting, father!
And you have long black locks—
a shock of hair!

Yes, I think, long locks like this belong on a male—
a bush of hair, a mane, a jungle, a tanglewood, a black forest,
the forest in every fairy tale:
forest of brambles
in which we lose our way.
The stepmother did this, the woman did this, the story tells us;
she cast us out; the king simply allowed it dumbly.
No—these woods are he.

❦ ❦ ❦

I stand by the stiff-backed waves
I stand by the venomous surf
and the birds unleash their yells
noon rages
the sea slides back and forth, green and high
and I am what I am
nothing is anything but what it is.
My mother loved another
and we've banned my mother's mother.
Now I am alone.

❦ ❦ ❦

I am in the belly of the whale—
Belly of my dreams.
If I were not here,
Weeds would be wrapped around my head;
I'd be lying on the floor of the sea.
But—am I swimming up or down?—
How do I find my way forth now,
Get to be vomited onto dry land?

❦ ❦ ❦

I have been rigged and launched, so
I must be a boat, said the boat.
Let me not be
a paper boat sailed down the drain.

Time
to find
a reason and
a rhyme—
to try
to climb
the ladder to
a poem.

A black duck can pounce straight up from the water.
A scaup staggers up little by
little—as I have fled in nightmares, wondering:
will they catch me by the feet before I am aloft?
This morning I started a pheasant.
Ah, what it took her to get up from the ground!
Her wings spanked the air: phewww rttt tt tt!
God help me, too, to wing up, flap up, somehow:
Phewww rtt tt tt!

I toss you this incense
swing to you this light burden of my head
tip it out to you
as, paddling toward the sea surface
I break through dream after dream,
each time thinking myself awake.

To fight
is almost the easiest part.
It is the search for the battlefield
that tries me.
I feel as though I were fighting in one of those
Shakespearian battles in which
the king protects himself by having a dozen or so warriors
wear his dress.
Which is the real king—whom must I challenge?

Here is the night.
Thud.
It sits on our shoulders.
And when we pass into sleep
it is whether we will it or not.
It is beyond our willing as the spring brooks racing with
one voice through the woods.

***

You are not at home to anyone, tell yourself.
    You are confronted by something like the end
of the world.
    The rocks headed toward you, or you toward them—
it doesn't matter which.
    Your hands, skilled perhaps (and t*his* doesn't matter)
hang by your sides, or are just on the wheel.
    Only your eyes are active.
    Your belly, although very much alive (as you will
know in an hour or so) sits very still, before the event.
    This is how one must be to write.

    Yes, the nose of the poet is pressed to the glass.
He is looking for something as momentous as the end
of the world. Or its beginning.
    He flaps to the ground, beating his head on sand,
or on rock, his mouth pecking questions.
    I am this poet.
    All eyes.
    My eyes are so wide I cannot see.
    I am beyond myself.
    I am the cart before the horse.

    "Keep out of the parlor!" they are bound to cry.
Of course.

ℊ

VIDA

1942-1953

ℊ

photo by Dorothy McWilliams
Barbara in Europe1949

I sit among green
But I think grey.
Overhead a bird like the swinging red painted cloth
bird-on-a-stick of my childhood
makes a circle, humming.
Under the swinging bird
I wait to awake.

I sit among green .
I snore with the toads
breathe in, breathe out
I mumble with the bumble
I sit under a swinging bird
and wait to see it
wait to hear it hum.

I wait not for the bird to come out of the bush
but for my eyes to see it
where it sits on a near branch

hops over leaves

I sit among a hundred birds
balanced on a hundred branches
and wait to know it
wait to see the flutter, the quick bird moves,
yellow brown red

On the branches open
the first bird flies up
Then I remark another who sits facing me
not three feet away—remarking me

It all begins to be visible
like those images that appear on paper if you brush
water on lightly.

This love I feel has become a bird that
hides behind leaf,
calls from the tree, wit wit,
but will not show itself,
plagues me from the bough with wit wit
but keeps itself hid,
walks round the bole of the tree
as I walk round.
Oh ghost that follows me round,
come out, come out!

♫♫♫

Each time it startles me
the new day
this striking of light from leaf
light from light
green speaks green
I walk the water
through a day like this
Noon is a flood
that bears us upon its breast
bears us all up.

At dusk
we are folded in
the wave gathers us
in its green paw
and we are worn by the night's motion
a sea-worm's labor
we are worn of our shape.

But dawn splashes us, startled, upon the
sand
the new day.

I like to remember a Persian miniature
an illuminated print of
a little figure praying in a thicket
while his horse, a little pale blue horse,
waits for him outside the thicket
head quietly down to crop the grass.

Like the traveller in a Japanese Noh play, I wait—
wait to meet, try to meet, the appropriate ghosts.
I don't know where to find them.
Or they won't speak, won't tell me their histories.
I wait and wait
to clasp hands
to listen and to speak.
I wait at various gates. I wait in all weathers
Lean out of the window far
but the ghosts recede.
I stare into faces in newspapers, animal's faces,
faces on buses, faces passing in the street.
"As face answers face in water, so the heart of man to
the heart of man"—but not for the bending over.
I hang above the stream. I wait for the image to form.
Monkeys parrots beetles drop coconuts oranges pebbles
into the water and the image won't form.

"*Thou wast...to me...*
A green isle in the sea, love..." Poe

The flood bore me to you. Curled in its paws, I
turned my eyes in your direction, and you had hardly
smiled your green smile when I fell upon you.
The flood advanced with me, let me drop, levelled out over
me, dragging out my locks (they stood out on end as though I were
hung by them from a peg on the wall, fairy-tale captive)—
and receded. I climbed to my knees and fell upon you, climbed
to my knees and fell upon you, smiling and frowning, and still
drowning. I then wandered you without eyes for you. Forgive me.
My life was still passing before my eyes.

♙♙♙

The ferris wheel
in the middle of the woods
stops
and my heart stops
The small lights rise
stop
and drop over into the thin air
as your mouth stops my mouth
and my circling heart
stops.

♫♫♫

Limbs on their rack
of bone twitch
for the dance,
find it not, fall
down. Dust
reshuffles the pack.

Each
again jumpy, the
little time he's
given,
thinks he hears
music,
far calls,
but takes it back,
falls, as
chattering from a slack
string
fall down
rare stones.

Is the music too far and faint
and queer
for the ear?
In tons and tons the bones
rain down here.

Teach us to stop listen stop look,
hold heart still
and hold back breath.
Hush—the music
gathers us out of death.

Still Life

Ovid tells of love-compelled ones
Who at the end of love's race
In place of their charmers embrace
Laurel tree or mulberry
And there go round it miserable.

I am one of these
Out of "Metamorphoses!"

Three stills give back this history, and mine.
As first—middle of the woods the setting:
One brought to a full stop by love of the stranger
As he alarms her, bathing.
She is caught in the act of stepping out of the water,
Freezes, foot in air,
And for this arrested moment they stare head-on,
Full glare.
See how he is impaled.
He has trespassed, with a step, with a glance,
In upon a mystery, in upon privacy.
In this moment before you
Pouting Cupid has him with the arrow.

I am one of these
Saucer-eyed stormer of mysteries.

He follows her as though she were his soul escaping.
See him, caught up in that posture, flailing, awry,
Limbs reaching out, the head thrust too far forward,
Hair streaming back, limbs dreaming as they fly, and aflame.
Transfixed in air, he is spent upon that element,
Burns there.

I am one of these—
Borne where the arrow please.

Last
See him with his fists full of snatched green
Stare at the trembling bush.
The shiny screen of flat petals
Trembles but gives no place.
Petals, fall apart! Bole and branches, split!
And Love, come out, come out!
His mouth is open as if to utter one interminable note.
Who is she?
I am my beloved. Now I cry: Who am I?

I am one of these
Without identities.

The Daughter

Andromeda
from her rocks
looks out to sea
with a glittering
fixity.

> Where does the beast
> crouch who's
> to devour me?

She scans the flat
water and complains:

> Twined in chains
> through my mother's pains,
> here I am—the feast.
> where is the beast?

Perseus' shadow
lightening the wave
causes her to color
causes her to rave:

> Who is this Perseus
> who drops from above
> on his airy feet
> speaking of love?

> Twined in chains
> through my mother's pains
> here I am: the beast
> will have me as its feast.

No wonder Perseus
passing over
had to drop down
to discover
was she
flesh and bone
or was she
figured in stone.

The labor of Perseus
is to engage
not the monster in its rage
but the maid
who, twined in her chains,
disdains
all aid.

Two Resolutions

I.   *"And the Lord sent fiery serpents among the people, and*
they bit the people...And Moses prayed...And the Lord
said unto Moses, Make thee a fiery serpent, and set it
upon a pole: and it shall come to pass that every one
that is bitten, when he looketh upon it, shall live."
Numbers 21

Flies up at my feet
A serpent swarm,
The sharp-toothed
Days of my youth.
Under hail of hissing,
Of venom-kissing
Mouths, I lay me down to sleep—

But would arise.
Rear before my eyes
The necessary spectre.
The harsh worm,
Sign of my days,
Is raised to a power:
I burn in its gaze
And begin to wake.

Fiery fact, strike
If I try to turn away.
Unwind your rattling
Entire burden and break
Into my dreams! Leave none
Intact!

II.   *"The piling up of the past upon the past goes on without*
      relaxation…In its entirety, probably, it follows us at every
      instant…We are dragging (it) behind us unawares."
      [Bergson]

                                                          This
pile on my back, this aging rider, this
I, cluck and whoa, makes mock of me,
ride a cock horse. When I'd
bolt I remember circus caricature:
clown with skeleton after
takes to his heels, and
wherever he goes, it follows, for
it's affixed to him; his
flight but excites the bones,
shakes up a deathly dance.

                                                          But
I'll not play your trotter to the grave,
old hump, poisonous one,
man of the sea; I mean to have you
answer to me one day.
You may, under my grappling hands,
play through your changes,
beast to beast to beast to beast,
grimace wrinkling
backward into grimace;
I'll see the succession out—

                                              For when there
clears at last before my squinted eyes your docile
smaller image—original guise—
old enemy, you'll answer what I ask:
where lies my liberty?

Over my head a wooden gull with wooden head
on creaking neck follows ship and eyes me.
I am sea-sick. Love-sick.
He follows ship.
I turn the pages of a book—not to look up,
the while the ship heads me across the
fish-heavy, the backward sliding sea.
Must I look you in your wooden eye, gull?
Fly to the captain for me. Ask him where this ship
is going.
I am sea-sick. Love-sick.

♫♫♫

My love lies over the ocean,
My love lie over the sea,
My little dog barks—
He doesn't recognize me!

For love has my tongue,
Love has my eyes—
There's little for him
To recognize.

Love has my left hand,
Love has my right—
If I come any nearer,
The dog will bite!

Love lies over the ocean,
Love lies over the sea!
Remember, oh remember me!

♪♪♪

I found my brother turned to a tree stump
on the lawn, turned to
moss
in the green of evening.
He was stalking a night hawk and
moving so patiently across the grass
that his feet turned grass,
his head turned moss, and
only his eyes
still moved.

Sea green evening.

♪♪♪

Complaint

Fie, the worm is in my branches again.
Where is the gardener?
My leaves despoil the garden;
The birds scream.
The keeper of this place
Is a sleeper,
Sleeps on, near by, while
The worm makes me his ladder and
Puts out my eye.

Dear girl,

     I wander. Call me home.

     Call home my eyes.

     They are locked in another's.

     They drown along the way, they are entangled,
bewitched.

     Transformations along the way.

     Merlin—I am locked in a tree.

     I turn to laurel—to tree to flower to stone

     lost in this magic garden, then in another, I am
turned to stone. The game of statues—freeze! Still-pond—
until you enter. Until you take me by strength. Claim me.

     It is always like seeing you after a long voyage.

     For the taste on my lips is foreign, scent in my
nostrils—and yours. A kiss of this sort, at midnight, at the
return. On your lips, wine, cigarettes, coffee. Homecoming.
You bring with you—clinging imperceptible to your garments,
flesh, mouth—a room, a street, a country.
Lucretius—disturbed tiny particles cling.
Like the breeze in from the sea. Cargo. Spices, perfumes, fruits.
An echo—a whisper—Where have you been, love?

     Call me back.

"Eu Cithaeron, why did you harbor me?" Oedipus

Eu Cithaeron—
Land out of which I might never have
Limped into this day which holds me now,
Sweet shade
Where I might still lie bound
Who am found
And lost,
Still glade
Where I might still lie
Still!

I set my crooked step to be caught
Thrashing in this day's snare
And I would wind me back
My track
But wind me where?
I squint back toward that ghostly time
And nothing shapes upon the noon-blind air of that
Shade where I might still lie bound
Who am found
And lost,
Still glade
Where I might still lie
Still.

Sunk is the moon,
The Pleiades are set;
Tis midnight; soon
The hour is past; and yet
I lie alone.

        Sappho

Midnight is gone.
The streets run empty to the rivers.
In the starless air
The electric signs shift, one rising
As the other sets, in place.
They do not mark the hours,
But I mark them. I
Lie here alone.

ꝯꝯꝯ

This love is rooted like the bramble:
All its green can be torn from the breast;
The plant seems to have been plucked out
Entire; it is nevertheless
Rooted through and through the very
Ground that has been scoured—
Thrusts again the flourishing briar
That bears tart berry, sweet flower.

ANNIE

1952

photo Louise Bernikow
Barbara Deming, 1979

Norma...a retrospective

When I lay down upon your body, I lay down upon the earth—
and had been walking too long upright, unsteady on my feet,
dizzy, but not knowing how to fall. When I moved my hand across
your body, I moved it across the unbounded sweet and zestful
earth: I had the illusion that beyond the bone of your hip I
could have moved my hand on and on and found you still.
When I fell down upon you, you received me (and I remember still)
as the earth receives again whatever is born of it—mother mother
To return to you after all this time is strange is sweet is to
sleep again after being too wakeful too long.

I am traveling light,
Am down to the bones,
And now that god who watches over those
A long way from home,
Watch over me.

I have hung have hung
On the hickory tree
All that ever covered me
And take the road,
And now some god
Turn me three times around
And set me upon the way—

A frightful way
And yet delightful:
The day is set
But there are brightnesses that decorate its wake,
Scattered light, star light,
But by this queer light
Foot can move,
Heart , even, can give a shout.
I put my left foot
Put my right foot out
And take this way.

And take this way,
And here's my joy:
To dance with all my might
Before this older than David's ark:
The Big Dipper up-ended
In a question mark.

Love shakes me.
Love has its hand upon me and with
Obstinate motions
Unmakes what I am.
It circles its seven times round me:
I am down.
Who says that love has gentle ways?
Awakened out of all order,
I am fire air earth water.

ઝઝઝ

An eye for an eye, love
A mouth for a mouth
Next me lie, love
I'll give you both

Next me lie, love
Limb by limb,
Each take the other's
Life from him

Let us touch, love
Let us go
If that much, love
Frightens you
Turn aside, then
Hide our eyes
And in parting
Sigh our sighs.

ক্ষক্ষক্ষ

"Rain, rain, go away."

If I love her lightly now,
Who knows how love might grow?
If I know not how it grows—
And know not where the wind blows
And know not where time goes
And know not why love chose
This time of this day
And this unfamiliar way—
Then I am love's, and not love mine,
And here is endless wondering.

Are we members one of another
Are these words so?

        If they are so, my breath
        Blow from you this death!

Is this metaphor?
Or is it more?

        If it is more, my prayer
        Tangle your life here!

Can lives touch
If love dares reach—
If one dares love another as one's self?

And can one dare this much?

Ghostly life within us,
Are the words plain?
Or is my straining prayer
Vain?

~

MARY

1957-1969

~

photo Judith McDaniel

Mary Meigs with a portrait of Barbara
Deming—1991

After my father died, I, one night, in a dream,
Entered the ground in which they had planted him.
I found him, not asleep, but lying at anchor, propped
In a narrow boat, on his elbows, as if rising in bed.
The ribs of the boat were his ribs, old wood,
And his head, toward me, was its figurehead.
A tangle of matted roots, his hair
Had sprouted thickly through the air.
Air, earth, or was it water? All here
Was one dark but transparent matter.
In awe again of parting with him, I dropped
To my knees. Despair of meaning in our lives
Fluttered in me. I groped to touch him. Unreasoning
Hope then thrust my hands
Into the thicket sprung from his brows.
The floating shaggy web embraced me;
I felt my blood race back and forth to me along the vine,
And my breath stop; the sour strong perfume
Of upturned earth choked my lungs;
And in the one harsh stroke
I felt my life renew, and woke.

Marriage

1.

Love is the falling rain,
Love is the following flood,
And love is the ark
With two of a kind aboard,
Love is the sequence of long days
At sea, without relief,
And love is the improbable
Return of the dove
Carrying in its beak
The green leaf.

2.

Our arms drew a circle
In which we lay
Charmed, awry.

Over our heads, the Bear
Set his glittering tread,
The Dragon slid, on fire,
Unremembered
Years away.

Our four legs, four arms
Moved in disarray—
But seeking order
Where on earth we lay.

3.

Marriage instructs us in death:
Kisses spend our breath,
Our spirits fly out of our mouths,
Our trembling stops, we fall still.
Marriage instructs us to smile at
Death's state which here we
Imitate.
Our two selves may scattered be,
Our married limbs together lie.
The knot they tie
Instructs us in eternity.

This is the hour
When the moth begins to seek,
The toad to utter its small cry
Which almost can be deciphered
As human speech, among the leaves,
And you and I,
Turning one to the other,
Each beyond the other's reach,
Try, too, for haven,
Try to speak.

✿✿✿

Which way is North, which way is South?
What are the words that blow out of my mouth?
Some god turns me three times round,
There's a new world to be found.

I spin deaf and I spin blind,
I spin mouth open in the wind,
There's a new world to be found,
The old world is here unwound.

Turn me till I am twice blind,
Turn all past times out of my mind,
When the curious motion dies,
Shut my mouth, open my eyes,

Give me something to make me wise.

1.

Lord, drop me to my knees,
I walk a crooked path.
Take from me these liberties,
Take from me my crooked staff,
And here
Where the old year
Falls
Through the air
Throw down
With the one wrath
Summer and this poor memory.
I would begin again.

Or can
A man
Wear green a second time?
Has this
Ever been?
Lord, make it so.
My own heart
Tells me No.

2.

Our Father who art hidden,
Hollow for us is the word with which we try
to speak Your name,
Your kingdom dim, Your will unknown,
Earth and its comforts all we know of haven.
Are You in fact our daily bread?
It must be. We forget it, as others forget us when
we are beyond reach.
Lead us not by the light alone of our own
vision. We overlook familiar marvels. Remind us of Your
power and Your glory over and over again.

3.

Now to break from sleep I try
I pray the Lord my soul to shake
I pray the Lord my dreams to wreck
I would wake before I die.

༺༺༺

Variations

Winter holds these woods within its vise.
The cold boughs creak like harness.   The ground
Is stiff as stone.   At the woods' edge
Jays call.   Their repeated cries
Wake the heart, as the flick of a nail
Wakes crystal: locked in winter, summer lies.

༺༺༺

Locked in winter, summer lies.
Gather your bones together.   Arise

Day puts forth its leaves upon night's stalk.
Stand.   Walk.

"Am I a God at hand?" Jeremiah

Pray for us.
One and true, God is
Each new day a new
God, abides with us
But hides from us who it is He is.
Pray for us.
He awaits us in unheard of places
With His despaired of graces.

∞∞∞

Once
I seemed to myself my own Maker.
When I sat up in the morning
Zest seemed to be
Born within my own breast,
Every move I made
I felt I made at will,
My every thought
Self-taught.
But now
Whatever were my spirits stand still.
My hands shake
My thoughts evaporate.
What power once caught me in its flood
So that my limbs
Seemed to swim?
Fathering spirit,
Breathe on me again!

⚛⚛⚛

My Muse has left me.
I sit here
Crouched as it were to speak
But—sit here in place.

I sit here in place.
I stare about the room.
I try to scare words
From the walls
With frowns.

I try to scare words from the walls.
I try to call back inspiration
With a stare.
I peer after it—
Face to the empty air.

⚛⚛⚛

Where are my words?
I bite the air

Earnest to speak
Unable to stir

Peering at vacancy
I sit here

Flesh and blood,
I would if I could
Be re-made
In finer mode.
I try to ask this
Of my neighbor.
We are as we are
And yet his doting
Or his doubtful stare
Turns what is
To air.
It is a hard labor
To hold the shape I'm given
As best I can
And look to no man—
Look to "heaven"—
For grace.

The heart, like the mind,
Is of fabric meant
To be stretched;
We are wretched unless
It bear a more than comfortable stress.
Yet we seek comfort
Though it binds us in wretchedness.
We sicken for God's kingdom
But contract our hearts upon less.

The years retreat
But, advancing, I grow thin.
The time I gain
Consumes me as I run.
Yet is there peace to be won.
The peace of God
Passes understanding.

Childhood is
Strenuously shed.
I am my own
Man.
But my gait's the gait
Of a skeleton.
Yet is there peace to be won.
The peace of God
Passes understanding.

Various demons circle round my head.
How shall I scatter them?
What charms can be said?
Somewhere I have read—
Or dreamed it—
Of a saint who, at prayer,
Moved his hands continually in the air,
To brush off like insects
Hovering unwanted thoughts.
They are best dismissed, perhaps,
With light gestures.
But these gestures
Are difficult rites.
Here are fantasies—yes,
I should stare
Through them, wave them away.
But they are my
Very own creatures.
How shall I scatter them?
What charm can I say?

❦

JANE

1969-1984

❦

Photo Judith McDaniel
Jane and Barbara , 1982
Sugarloaf Key

1.

Each night I cling to you—
A floating spar.
Do we drift landward? A star
That trembles slightly lights
The hurrying waves that
Carry us along.
Will it light us home, do you think?
Are we carried toward or
Away from the darkling shore?

2.

My love is water.
I swim in her arms,
Struggling toward what new land?
Visions of it catch at my mind
As, buffeted, sustained,
I change, I change.
Life as it has been drowns,
The life I swim to groans: "Begin"
And I am born: Her glimmering smile
Draws me out of my skin.

3.

As we embrace
It seems to my dreaming mind
You hold me in six welcoming arms
Not two—
In dancing motion like the arms
Of Shiva, clasping me through and through
My flesh to find out who it is I am.
And now your two eyes have become
One gleaming one.
Its deep glance discovers
All that I am.
You enter my soul.

I lie at the bottom of my spirit's well
And try to still my breath
And still my heart
That staggers in my side
Like an uneven wheel.

Above me, agitation of the waters.
Some of this motion is life,
Some is death.
Each is mistaken for the other,
In panic, often, that turns to wrath.
I see that wrath cut back
Everything new, green, that we try to begin.

And will life or will death prevail?
My fear is asking the question
And the answer to fear, of course, is: Death.

I lie at the bottom of my spirit's well.
If I lie quiet here
Can I elude my fear?

*** ***

Behind her the sea the sea hisses—
A serpent in a new skin.
Each altering moment it sloughs from it an old
And glistens in another skin again.
And she and she—
Dances to its many-throated
Its never-for-a-minute silent song ("Listen, listen!")
And sings, herself: Here
I mean to dance away my fear.
It binds me like a jacket I have worn too long.
(Yes, I hear your song.)
I'll slip it from me
As you slip your watery coats
And dare be naked, known
As whatever self I am
Or I become.
And grimaces (for a moment doubting this?)
But dances on.

❦ ❦ ❦

I.

Beyond the field in which I am lying now—

The shining yellow flower of the strawberry at my hand—

I can look into the woods of Death.

My friends are gathering there—

George Edna Burling Friedel Polly Win

    Ron Cummings and Marion A.J.

       Nennie

           Ockene

              Giovanna

                  Henry

                      Edmund—

How near they are!

A few steps and I could be among them.

Would be now if, waking in a hospital last Fall,

Battered, appalled, I had not fought for breath,

Fought to hold this remaining ground.

Mending, I lie naked among the flowering grasses, in the

sun,

And stare toward the break at the edge of the field

                  where the woods begin—

A dazzle of green upon green.

How near you are!   Still seen,

Still heard, I can touch each one of you still.

In the past.   But the past, for me, is present, it is now.

      No, not for you.

      For you, now is the utterly new.

      Thought fails me here—

II.

As my poem broke, I learned that you are dead, too, Paul.
Day after day, now, I find myself trying to speak with you.
I have no words. Words, too, are in the ground.
But with gestures formed in our soul before words were found, I
turn myself in your direction—turn, with your turning, to face
what is too new to name.
"Lo!"—as you have written. *That* word exists—the first?
May we be brave enough to be changed.
Each one of us. May each one of us learn to be born.
I stare toward the woods where my friends are gathering.

※ ※ ※

Illness holds me by the ankle.
I lie in its hand as in a trap.
And where's my patience?
This grip will loosen, but not until
Day after day after day has lapsed.
In this captivity, patience must be my bread.
But where is patience found?
How is this bread ground?
I'll grind it of my bones, I think I know—
Between the stones that are the slow
Days and nights I undergo to earn escape.
I'll learn to grind hope to its finest grain,
And learn to learn this each day over again.

Spirit of love
That blows against our flesh
Sets it trembling
Moves across it as across grass
Erasing every boundary that we accept
And swings the doors of our lives wide—
This is a prayer I sing:
Save our perishing earth!

Spirit that cracks our single selves—
Eyes fall down eyes,
Hearts escape through the bars of our ribs
To dart into other bodies—
Save this earth!
The earth is perishing.
This is a prayer I sing.

Spirit that hears each one of us,
Hears all that is—
Listens, listens, hears us out—
Inspire us now!
Our own pulse beats in every stranger's throat,
And also there within the flowered ground beneath our feet,
And—teach us to listen!—
We can hear it in water, in wood, and even in stone.
We are earth of this earth, and we are bone of its bone.
This is a prayer I sing, for we have forgotten this and so
The earth is perishing.

❦ ❦ ❦

Death Song
(To Bessie Breuer, 1894-1975)

You are in the earth.
I lie in bed, knees to my chest
(as we were buried when death
was known to be the Mother),

not quite thinking of you—my thoughts stand
still—but dying a little myself.
With you.
I don't get up.
There's nothing
that I want to do.
My days stop.

"In the beginning was the listening," a woman has
now dared to say—though at your funeral
they quoted JOHN.
I try to listen—or lying stiller still,
to listen to a listening.
I can't hear,
try to hope.

My body remembers your knobby skeletal
body in my arms.
The nurse had propped you in a chair and,
in a delirium, I think,
you tried and tried again and tried again and tried
again to stand.
To keep you from toppling forward,
I put myself in your way,
catching you under the arms each time, your
thin breast, like a lover's, pressed
against my breast. In this wrestling I think your greeting
to death passed into my bones.
I take it as a gift,
though I am now undone.

You are in earth, death, in the Mother,
and, knees to my chest, I too
wait in Her—Death Mother, Life Mother,
the Old One, the Listener—as you must be waiting—to be heard,
to have Her bring us forth again,
and name us—
Who are we now?

Love Song

I want to try to tell you what I feel
When you and I like naked together:
                              The walls
Of this house fall—
We embrace in the wide air.
Near branches (lilac), clouds in streamers,
The glimmering stars,
Become one seamless garment that we wear.
Voices of crickets take small stitches in it;
The pattern of their airy cries is pricked
Upon our flesh.
Wind turns the leaves of the lilac upon their stems
And this rush of leaves is our breath—
Taken between kisses.
As day and dark and no and yes are shaken together, we
Rock each other awake.
                              With her quick
Quiet leap, our cat comes to the bed.
She likes the way we smell now in our heat,
Stares at us, then lies down at our feet
To hum an elated song.
Does she, too, dream as she hums
That all life is one?

This hugging has unlocked our bodies
We exchange limbs
My mouth now sits on a small branch
Of the starfruit tree outside your window
And sings:
Am I her mouth or mine?
Are these my hands or hers
Among the summer grasses
Fingers tangled?
Is this my tongue that has found the sweet salty
Very center of the earth—
Which as it turns
Flings us akimbo yet together
And also turning
In slow
Rings and rings and rings?

Our love, like the new moon,
Lies at last within the old moon's arms
And grows again.
Lone night after night we had been
Without its light—this grace withdrawn.
Shaken with tears, we spoke our loss—
Admitting what was bitter, bitter,
With this burst water
Love was born again.
Again I swoon upon your mothering breast,
Again the white crescent of your body
And my body are joined, and blessed.

Waking Up Writing a Poem

A faraway rooster utters a spark to be blown into dayblaze.
The January wind circles our house with a voice like surf.
And now the trash collectors begin to crash their way
Out of last night's dreams and down our block.
You open one eye and shut it again smiling.
I ask, "Can you give me a rhyme for 'dayblaze'?"
"Heydays," you yawn.
Yes, these are heydays, dear friend—
My days with you—however difficult.
And it's a merry luxury
To wake by your side.

I'm listening to our old dog
beneath the couch
dreaming.
She barks softly
and distantly.
Is she in the hills
young again
following some delicious scent?
(her paws move in her sleep)
Or does she dream of now
and it is age with all
its confusing afflictions
that she is trying to outrun?

In the window our cat
whiskertips
probing the view, receives what is about to happen.
She watches the yellow rose we've planted
that climbs among the fruit tree branches.
Can her gaze capture one of the very moments
when the green shoot grows?

I close my eyes.
Now, then, to come—
which is most real?
The answer whispers through me:
alive in us
are all three,
all three.

Gorgons, unruly gorgons,
With eyes that start, with curls that hiss—

Once
I listened to the fathers' lies,
Took their false advice:
I mustn't look at you, I'd turn to
Stone.

But now I meet your clear furious stare and
It is my natural self that I become.
Yes, as I dare to name your fury
Mine.
Long asleep,
It writhes awake.

Ssisters, ssisters—of course they dread us.
Theirs is the kingdom
But it is build upon lies and more lies.
The truth-hissing wide-open-eyed rude
Glare of our faces—
If there were enough of us—
Could show their powers and their glories
To be what they merely are and
Bring their death-dealing kingdom
Down.

This is a song for gorgons—
Whose dreaded glances in fact can bless.
The men who would be gods we turn
Not to stone but to mortal flesh and blood and bone.
If we could stare them into accepting this,
The world could live at peace.

I sing *Our* song for those with eyes that start,
With curls that hiss.
Our slandered wrath is our truth, and—
If we honor this—
Can deal not death but healing.

I sing: This will be done!

I sing: Their kingdom *wane!*

What are you afraid of, my friend and beloved?
Why do you lie so warily in our bed
Under my inquiring hands?
Are you afraid that my hands would like to tame you?
Have you forgotten the odd looks we exchanged
Years ago, before we even spoke?
Didn't we recognize one another in those glances—
And recognize, too, our own selves,
Kindred selves—
In each the same will to elude
Captivity—to grow wild,
If we could, if we could?
Isn't this why year after year we remembered each other?
And isn't this why finally we sought each other out?
And if I *could* tame you,
Wouldn't I by that act
Douse in you the very spirit that moved me
And still moves me to choose you—
Unruly spirit my own unruly self delights to live near
And (to catch added courage for unruliness)
Would also sometimes like to touch.

Death Song

To Consuelo Kanaga (1894-1978)

And now
Consuelo has gone.
I tell myself: Don't grieve.
She hadn't been at ease in her ailing body
For years,
Didn't want to live on and on—
Breath no longer freely taken,
Taken on the rack,
And gut wrecked by cancer.
When we last talked, she said,
"I think I'm getting stronger!"—
Not telling this as good news,
Bewailing it.
Consuelo, no, I won't grieve.
But I weep: Thank you for your life,
You are one of my mothers.
I weep: Where are you—now that you have been
Sprung from your jail—friend of my heart?
Your dying shakes me into a time outside of time,
And I wake here not knowing what my senses tell me.
I weep, startled as a child newly born,
Overwhelmed.

* * *

For Consuelo Kanaga (1894-1978)

I stare out my door at a young palm
With curly fronds the wind is in—
Stare at the shaken tree and
Remember that you are dead. Again
Questions flood my mind:
Death, what do you make of us?
Where have you taken my friend?
Then I let go of questions—
Let them be tossed in all this ragged
Shuddering green.
The wind is a light storm wind.
I wait for the storm to draw near.
Just there
Behind the dancing tree
Thunder lightly growls.
In your voice!
It is in your beloved voice,
My never-to-be-lost
My everlasting friend!

A Catechism

If you believe in one God, a Father Almighty,
What are you letting yourself forget?
If you believe that everything
Proceedeth from The Father and The Son,
Whom have you agreed to scorn?—
Whose body do you cast
Out of memory
As though in shame?

If your mind refuses these questions,
Ask them of your flesh.
Was it at a father's breasts that you suckled?
Was it from a father's womb that you swam?

❧ ❧ ❧

Hallowed Be

We have been taught to say at our prayers
"Hallowed be Thy name".
What do these familiar words
Actually mean?
Don't they mean that God has yet to be
Known by a name that is whole?
To call the Maker-of-all-that-is "Our Father"
Is droll. We know the facts of life.
More than droll. An act of
Violence against half of us—cause for wrath.
And the time has come round to speak this truth.

I live with a cat who
likes to dance.
I once
set her on my shoulder as I
danced a slow prance.
Now
each day
she asks
with a small cry
for me to take her up and
step away.

She hums as we go—
her tail a furry wand that stirs the air
in solemn figure-eights—as though
she'd bring a turnaround to all our lives
and all we think we know.

Cat, what dance is this?
The Bible raves of Man's dominion over
everything that moves.
Is this a dance to dance an end
to all dominion?
I meet your glance that's shining
in a mirror as we pass.
It says: Yes! Yes!

For Barbara Smith

Your first words to me—"We've
Been in the same struggles"—
Generous words
For I steal rest that you cannot.
But yes, our lives join.
I keep dreaming a poem to you
Which rejoices in this.

My voice shakes, though.
In place of words
I find tears in my throat.
They have been locked in me
But now burst.
So much has been taken from us.

But we will take it back.
I sit next you again—
My hands in yours.
They took this: our right to touch.
Black, white,
Woman, woman.
We take it back
We take it back.

A Call

We've battened our house against
A hurricane that's gathering,
Whirls near;
Left one small window open to allow ourselves
This much air to breath
And now we're inside our one-eyed house,
Waiting.

It's later. Night. Lamps out.
I sit up in bed in
The unfamiliar
Tight-fitting dark—
Get to my feet.
Shouldn't we do more than wait?
I call to you:
Shouldn't we gather, too?
Shouldn't we, too, whirl?

These winds birth reveling energies
No one can leash.
Let's dare, then, to feel at one with them—
Turn about, too, in the dark,
Spread out our hands and stir the night air—
Musing, as we do, on all that *needs* disturbing.
Minds set in deadly rigor,
That can't change a deadly course—
We'll disturb them into
New ways of seeing.
Let's turn about and about and about,
Setting *our* minds wheeling, too;
Gathering within the gathering storm
Our own force.

A Song For Those Ill With Jealousy Of Women

We all give birth. Or can.
No need for jealousy.
Not one of us can invent life
And to each of us—woman or man—
New life
In one form or another
Is given again and again
For us to bring to birth
If we choose.
And all this life is one.
We are all branches on the one vine.
I don't mean Jesus.
Jesus was a beautiful man—
A lovely branch upon the vine—
But the vine is Nature herself, who is both she and he,
Everchanging and everlasting, alive in each of us.
No need for jealousy.
We all give birth. Or can. A child
Takes form within a mother's
Not a father's body
But once born
Seeks its form still
And needs to know that it is not alone in this—
Remembers how within the womb
Another heartbeat not its own
Beckoned it on.
Each one of us can learn
To beckon others
Beckon our own selves
To continue to be born
Upon the vine.
No need for jealousy.
Has the vine need to be jealous of the vine?

The sweet night waits for you, Mother.
The dark trees quietly stand.
This house which you have made your house
Utters its small night sounds
And waits for the sigh of your last breath.
Life has become a puzzle to you.
"What? What?" you ask.
And then you ask, "What is it?" It is
Death that stands near, Mother; but don't fear it.
It waits to lay on you a friendly hand.

*** *** ***

The leaves are talking
They are telling all the days of your life, Mother
They turn and turn on their many stems
At the window of your room
Do you hear them, I wonder?
You stare at something in the air between us
I can't see
Is it your death you study—
Or these leaves of your life?
Or is Death in fact our lives
Turned, told, retold
Until their truth is clear?
Mother, the leaves are talking, talking
Do you hear them—
Talking on the tree of Life, of Death,
Of Life.

EPILOGUE

photo by Quentin Deming
Barbara Deming 1984

A Song To Pain

(Written the night before my operation for cancer,
March 28, 1984)

This is a song to pain—
Which sometimes bites me,
Sometimes burns,
And sometimes knocks from a distance,
Makes me grunt a half-tune
A half-tune to pain
It goes: hu – ah, hu – ah
It asks: Explain
It asks my inner-most being to explain.

This is a song of grunts and groans,
A song of moans
Song of the turning axis of my life
Which strives —hu! – ah!
Against the grain
Strives to cross and recognize
This – hu! difficult last line –
                              ah!

(Next lines written July 25, 1984, in the night)

AND NOW MY SPIRIT GUIDES
HAIL ME AND SMILE
I'VE SUNG MYSELF BEYOND
THIS LIFE'S PALE

photo by Quentin Deming

Jane, Barbara and Mary
just before her death in 1984

ACKNOWLEDGEMENTS

"Still Life" and "Two Resolutions" appeared in Chimera, Summer, 1946. "The Flood Bore Me To You" and "The Daughter" appeared in Wakes 8, Autumn, 1949. "Merrygoround" appeared in Perspective, Winter, 1950. "Eu Cithaeron" appeared in The Paris Review, Summer, 1956. "An eye for an eye, love" appeared in The Paris Review, September, 1956. "Which way is North," "Lord, drop me to my knees," and "I am travelling light" appeared in Voices, May-August, 1958. "Variation on a Poem by Sappho" and "Love Shakes Me" appeared in Voices, May-August, 1959. "After my father died" appeared in Liberation, January, 1961. "Give us this day," "Our father," and "Now to break from sleep" appeared in Catholic Worker, May, 1963. "Am I a god at hand?" appeared in The Peace Calendar, 1968. "Our arms drew a circle" and "Marriage instructs us in death" appeared in WIN, January, 1971. "Let us touch, love," "If I love her lightly now," "This is the hour," "This love is rooted like the bramble," "Love is the falling rain," "My love is water," and "As we embrace" appeared as "Love Poems" in We Cannot Live Without Our Lives, Grossman Publishers, 1974. "Limbs on their rack," "Winter holds these woods within its vise," "Variation," "Various demons circle round my head," "I lie at the bottom of my spirit's well," "Behind her the sea hisses," "Illness holds me by the ankle," "Beyond the field in which I am lying now—," "Spirit of Love," appeared as "Prayers" in We Cannot Live Without Our Lives, Grossman Publishers, 1974. "A Song for Gorgons" appeared in Reweaving the Web of Life: Feminism and Nonviolence, edited by Pam McAllister, New Society Publishers, 1982. "Have been not admitting it all to be present, and given," "Remember: Descent into my parents' living room," "To fight," "Love Song," "For Barbara Smith," "I live with a cat who likes," "This hugging has unlocked our bodies," and "We've battened our house against" appeared in We Are All Part of One Another: A Barbara Deming Reader, edited by Jane Meyerding, New Society Publishers, 1984. "Love shakes me" appeared in A Humming Under My Feet, The Women's Press, England, 1985.